D0099555

Graphics in Motion

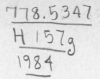

Graphics in Motion

From the Special Effects Film
to Holographics

John Halas

VAN NOSTRAND REINHOLD COMPANY
New York Cincinnati Toronto London Melbourne

First published in the United States in 1984
Copyright © 1981 by Verlag F. Bruckmann KG, München
Library of Congress Catalog Card Number 83-14803
ISBN 0-442-23505-4

A novum press book, produced with the cooperation of
novum gebrauchsgraphik
Printed in the German Federal Republic

Van Nostrand Reinhold Company Inc.
135 West 50th Street
New York, New York 10020

Van Nostrand Reinhold Company Limited
Molly Millars Lane
Wokingham, Berkshire RG11 2PY, England

Van Nostrand Reinhold
480 Latrobe Street
Melbourne, Victoria 3000, Australia

Macmillan of Canada
Division of Gage Publishing Limited
164 Commander Boulevard
Agincourt, Ontario M1S 3C7 Canada

16 15 14 13 12 11 10 9 8 7 6 5 4 3 2 1

Library of Congress Cataloging in Publication Data
Main entry under title:
Graphics in motion.
English and German.
Reprint. Originally published: München:
Bruckmann, 1981.
Bibliography: p. 185/186.
Includes index.
1. Cinematography – Special effects.   2. Computer
graphics.   3. Television graphics.   4. Holography.
I. Halas, John.
TR858.G7 1984   778.5'2345   83-14803
ISBN 0-442-23505-4 (pbk.)

Contents

Introduction

The design profession in perspective

The development of graphic design dates from the invention of photography some hundred and fifty years ago. Since then, owing to the turbulent changes of social adjustment, the function and position of the designer has been subjected to continuous reorientation. With the camera being used as a creative visual instrument, man's vision gradually extended beyond the narrow limits of the human eye.

As time went on, the graphic designer and the photographer learned how to employ each other's techniques and to enrich each other's profession. The basic tools of the graphic designer – pencil and brush – began to be amplified with the use of light effects, distorted views and manifestations of tone values from negative to positive shades. In fact, by the beginning of this century, our forefathers had enough stimulus to depart from a style of narrow representation and realism and to adopt an approach of imaginative symbolism. This substantially transformed the graphic design profession.

Later, as the manufacturing industries grew and education improved, mass production and mass consumption raised the standard of living. These economic and social developments created more opportunities for the graphic designer. The practice became professional, rendering its services to the advertising industries and marketing, public information and last but not least, the publishing and printing industries which, in their turn, experienced a most interesting technical advance. Mass communication had also entered its first phase.

During the Bauhaus period in the early twenties, a far broader view of the design profession was taken. A constructive relationship was established with architecture, theatre, the fine arts and once again with its close ally – photography. It also enriched itself by a wider use of materials, such as plastics, new colour inks, projected reflectors, reflected lights and convex mirrors.

By this time, another important influencing factor had arisen: As static photography evolved into cinematography, the borderline of function between the visualiser of moving pictures and the graphic designer working with static images had become somewhat blurred. The Cubists, Dadaists and futuristic movements coming from Italy and France also provided some stimulus and inspiration in the search for a new dimension. Artists and designers like Eggeling, Richter, Fischinger and in Bauhaus, Marcks and Moholy-Nagy, experimented with moving designs which became an important element in contemporary design.

Looking back on this era, over half a century ago, dramatic inventions and changes have been made since. In the electronics industry transmission technologies were improved by introducing the computer, the transistor, videoscope and disc as well as space satellites. Television spread around the world and mass communication became global; the science of cybernetics was established. Thanks to the progress made, education further expanded on both adult and junior levels. The graphic design profession, in the meantime, settled down to a peaceful coexistence with the photographic industry and began to explore the use of the optical lens.

The visual potential offered by the television and video industries, film-strips, slide, tape, overhead projectors, cassetted visual aids, back and front projection systems, computer terminals and laser and holographic methods, mean that the graphic design profession has become far more complex and requires not only a change in the methods used but also reconsideration on all levels. One of the basic dangers which the graphic design profession faces today is the fact that the public attitude is changing constantly, sometimes even more quickly than the profession. The development of cinematography and by its side the electronics industry, together with kinetic art and television, have brought about a generation whose visual perception is much more acute and instantaneous than their parents'. Verbal literacy has given way to visual literacy.

This results in simultaneous observation or multiple awareness of visual contact in one's environment.

As with most changes affecting our lives, artists are the first to observe them and to give expression to them. Way back in 1912, the Italian painter Boccioni and the French painter Delaunay exhibited simultaneity by showing faces, cars, furniture etc., in different positions and with different colour rotations on the same canvases. The philosophy of the simultaneous was already in existence. The human consciousness of things happening in different parts of the globe at the same time was already being felt, even before the arrival of television. This consciousness was motivated by rapid travel, the telephone, telegraph and the wireless as well as by the rapidly expanding circulation of newspapers and magazines.

The influence of multiple awareness can be observed not only in art, but also in the timing of every moving picture. One need only compare programmes produced a few decades ago to the ones made today to realise how image absorption has speeded up. There was a trend just a few years ago when typography and layouts also responded to this influence. The photomontage, the multiplicity of images, interlocked double canvas, fluid poetry and multi-screen projection are some examples of this trend. Fortunately, the convention has now been totally absorbed into visual communication as a whole and there is nothing new about the effect of its speed or in its fascination among the visualisers of today. What is required is an inspiring and imaginative interpretation – a recreation of the means of communication which simultaneity brought about.

The worrying aspect in design therefore, is the fact that while we are rapidly approaching the next century, we have hardly caught up with this one. It appears that there is now a necessity for better educational preparation for the tools associated with the new media, more creative enterprise, and a greater moral responsibility towards universal problems since graphic design has become one of the important tools of communication, embracing all aspects of human activity and conditions.

In this book, I intend to provide information on the range of tools at the disposal of the contemporary designer, some already in daily use, such as computer and video graphics and some in the process of development, such as lasers and holography.

Finally, we should not ignore the fact that some 30% of all graphic designers are already using some electronic aid in the form of audio-visual equipment, and some 20% are employed by the television companies' graphics departments throughout the world.

New design concepts

For several decades, there have been fundamental problems in bringing together those who work with static design and those whose designs become mobile. There is no doubt that both sides contribute effectively to visual communication and information in their own particular way. The time has now come to understand each other's problems more, as new methods of production and new tools are coming into use. Today, an inter-related knowledge of what is available in audio-visual techniques and what new potentials are possible for the design profession, is essential.

There are a few main points related to these problems which should not be forgotten:

The availability of audio-visual media techniques and their aesthetic potential;

the scale of the designers' contribution to films, TV, video and computer industries;

the question of how design education should go about changing from old established to contemporary lines and contemporary thinking.

The new potential challenge lies with the solutions to these problems.

In the meantime, one should not forget that the instruments of TV, cinema and video are cold, dead objects without the actual pictures which they reproduce. The question therefore is: Who should visualise the actual pictures on the screen?

Writers cannot create pictures; they can only imply them in writing. Electrical engineers cannot produce pictures; they can only convey them. Producers cannot make pictures; they can only arrange to have them made. It is the visualisers who have the responsibility. Visualisers can be directors, scenic designers or graphic designers or in fact a new breed – a combination of all three. It requires a new sense and a somewhat different discipline from past graphic performances. These are the prerequisites:

To be able to relate individual pictures to each other in order to represent an idea as a whole;

to communicate ideas in space and time;

to understand motion mechanics;

to be able to relate sound with motion;

to have a sense of timing;

to apply graphic organisation to technical needs;

to be able to use light adequately as raw material.

For many designers this means "unlearning" certain rules attached to static designs, especially to typography; for others it is a question of adopting new ones. The essential difference lies in the fact that in addition to design sense, when one is creating moving designs for TV, cinema and video, one also needs a fundamental understanding of how moving design works and how it can be processed through the various technical stages onto video tape and film material. It is essential here to realise that we are dealing with many different design languages:

1. Static design mainly processed through print.

2. Moving design exposed mainly on film and tape for cinema and TV screens.

Static design has its root in a basic organisation of forms, composition and typography and with it we strive to achieve an impression for instantaneous appreciation: an immediate impact. It can be observed at leisure in the onlooker's own time since the result is presented in a fixed position, mostly reproduced in the form of print.

In its fluid state, a design is subject to the passage of time. Each segment of design may appear for a fraction of a second only. What matters is the accumulation; the total impression. What lies in between two designs may be more important than the basic work itself. In this respect the designer's work acquires a close relationship with other disciplines which are also subject to the passage of time for their expression; for example ballet and music. Design in motion can be most effective when it succeeds in establishing a close and harmonious relationship with these other forms and achieves a rhythmical parallel with them. It is certainly less attractive and its potential value unexplored if the relationship between music and choreographic opportunities is neglected or unbalanced. Design in movement relies on these additional factors beyond the value of the design itself.

All movement is constantly dependent on the kinetic principle. Great masters of motion on stage, Pawlowa and Nijinskij for instance, knew by instinct and practice how to manipulate their bodies in space, being continually subjected to the forces of gravity. Their art consisted of giving expression through the movement of their bodies against the pull of the earth's gravitational forces. Like so many thousands of first-class dancers, they knew how to make good use of time and gravity. A design conceived in motion must overcome the same problems.

Unlike a static design which cannot change its shape, a moving design is capable of frequent changes. This transformation can acquire an aspect of metamorphosis. An animated shape, for instance, can move through the air and descend to the earth much more slowly than a living body, should the designer wish it to do so. A moving design therefore is not subject to physical laws to the same extent as a living body. This experience provides a sense of liberation for the audience and an endless opportunity for the designer to develop his art in space and rhythm in a wider dimension.

In conclusion, the designer of a static object expresses his work in concrete form, creating a formal composition which is a still life. It is totally self-contained, and although the printing and reproductive processes are an influencing factor, his work will appear as near to the original as possible.

The work of the TV and film designer, on the other hand, is fluid and dynamic. Most of the designs are prepared to respond to the passage of time and space and will be appreciated in the passage of time by an audience. Often the designer's work will be assembled at the last stages of the process – on the cinema screen, on the TV tube and on the computer terminal. That is where the final judgment will take place. This process of visualisation through motion in space, through light, is the new challenge to us all.

It is logical that reference should be made here to other professions apart from photography, which have direct influence on, and relationship with, graphic design and the element of movement in work. We are of course mostly concerned with the "representation" of a moving image and not the actual performance of it. This is the case with other forms of activity such as ballet, movement in plastic arts, the relationship between physical, psychological and biological movement, and movement in the arts in general, as well as real movements in the plastic arts in the kinetic sector. In the role of graphic design in the media, the audience is involved as a spectator and not as a participator, although to a certain point it is essential not only to raise its interest but also to engage its emotions. There is, however, a very strong relationship between fluid graphic design and kinetics for several reasons. They meet in the indispensable stage of isolating the basic sense data – colour, lines, tones and now movement. The evolution of the element of movement as sense data has influenced painting, sculpture and architecture to the same extent as has been the case with graphic design. In fact it has resulted in an entirely new art termed "kinetic", which has played such an important role in the world of plastic arts for the last fifty years.

It is essential that one should consider the relationship with these allied professions as well as to trace the influences in the present stage of developement, which could lead to a better understanding and appreciation of the techniques of "graphics in motion".

Physiology of Graphics in Motion

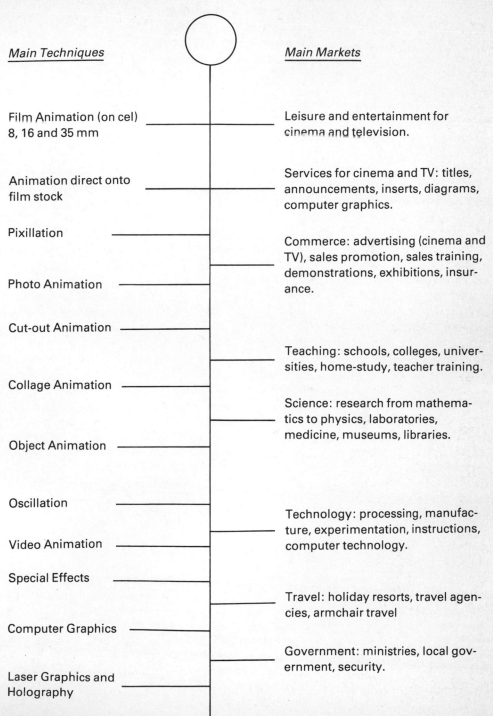

Main Techniques

Film Animation (on cel)
8, 16 and 35 mm

Animation direct onto
film stock

Pixillation

Photo Animation

Cut-out Animation

Collage Animation

Object Animation

Oscillation

Video Animation

Special Effects

Computer Graphics

Laser Graphics and
Holography

Main Markets

Leisure and entertainment for
cinema and television.

Services for cinema and TV: titles,
announcements, inserts, diagrams,
computer graphics.

Commerce: advertising (cinema and
TV), sales promotion, sales training,
demonstrations, exhibitions, insur-
ance.

Teaching: schools, colleges, universities, home-study, teacher training.

Science: research from mathematics to physics, laboratories,
medicine, museums, libraries.

Technology: processing, manufacture, experimentation, instructions,
computer technology.

Travel: holiday resorts, travel agen-
cies, armchair travel

Government: ministries, local government, security.

Film Graphics

"The Wizard's Son", 1981.

Direction: John Canemaker,
Phoenix Film/USA.

The meaning of film graphics is the application of movement to graphic images for a specific objective. Moving graphics are subjected to a number of technical processes not inherent in a static design such as an illustration, a poster or a brochure. Consequently, an element of movement necessitates an understanding of film techniques, motion dynamics, motion mechanics and timing. All these factors inevitably multiply the production period of a static design, sometimes as much as ten times.

There have been many specific developments during the 75 years of film graphics. At the start of the century, it was only possible to move black lines on a white ground or white lines on a black ground. Soon after the introduction of animated film by Emile Cohl in Paris, and after the development of moving comic strips, primarily through the work of the American, Winsor McCay, film graphics rapidly progressed. However, it was still only possible to manipulate movement in two dimensions. It was not until the invention and use of transparent celluloids (soon after World War I) that it was possible to divorce the backgrounds from the foregrounds and animate moving figures in perspective. The figures were drawn on paper and traced onto the transparent celluloids. By painting them on these transparencies, they became opaque shapes. The animation could now be manipulated to and fro in perspective, creating an illusion of three-demensional motion. The whole background could be seen through the transparent celluloid with the exception of such areas where the opaque shapes were laid over them. The camera exposed these combined pictures one by one on a 35 mm negative film and, when developed, a smooth animated picture emerged. The skill of the background artist, the animator and the cameraman were thus combined.

From the early Disney productions to the latest advertising films this technique has hardly changed in principle. During the early fifties, however, there was a rapid movement away from the use of cel animation. Designers felt that the use of hard defined outlines for the animated figures and flat painted surfaces to colour them, had straight-jacketed them from expressing a freer graphic image. Texturized animation was born out of this new movement, as well as a great many other approaches, among them painting the drawing directly onto the surface of the actual raw film. Today, there are innumerable techniques and approaches at the service of the film designer. With the application of electronics and automated processes, a whole range of further techniques has been introduced into this field. They will be explained in subsequent chapters.

In film graphics the visual approach cannot be divorced from the other elements which make up the final result. Moving design never works in isolation. It is always combined with such basic necessities as story-telling, words spoken with varying degrees of emphasis, and with the sound track which may contain all kinds of noises, special effects, music or silence, or a wide range of cinematographic devices. This includes object animation, i. e. animation with puppets, sand, glass, wood, pastels, collage with paper cut-outs or photographs, or it may be combined with actual live-action photography. In fact, there is an endless variety of possible combinations of these elements, provided there is a clear objective to be achieved and the method chosen is within the technical feasibility of the moving picture medium. Among the prime necessities, especially for commercial exploitation in full-length features and commercial films, is the creation of a mood and emotion. The question of how to create a mood or strong emotional impact is very important since without these a film, no matter what technique is employed, could become ineffective. So far, it has been found that an emotional approach pays far greater dividends than an intellectual one, if a product is to be sold or the general public entertained.

But in order to utilise any potential – design skills, artistic capabilities, good graphic organisation in typography, competent animation – in film graphics, it is necessary to conceive these elements with an expert sense of timing. These are qualities also required in TV graphics, but the emphasis is placed on exploiting the greater flexibility of film material and the inherent graphic possibilities of optical effects which are not always available in other media. Richer textures in background and in the design of characters are also plus factors. But the main progress, compared with only a decade ago, lies in the extremely wide range of graphic design styles which is now possible in film graphics.

There is practically no limit to stylistic expression in film and TV graphics from abstract avant-garde conception to representational forms. The limitations may exist only in the capability of the designer. This also applies to the optical film effects. The camera lens can be a wonderful instrument for visual imagination. Double exposure, superimposition and graduated tone effects, contribute to design values that only the medium of film will achieve.

The techniques of film graphics are widely ranged. It is a comparatively easy activity at design college level, since it is possible to produce movement on the surface of 16 mm or 35 mm film stock and to play it back immediately on a projector without going through the customary laboratory process of developing and processing the film. One is able to check, observe and study motion mechanics instantly without involving a photographic camera. The spread of simpler forms of equipment like the Super 8 mm film also encouraged young designers to understand the mechanics of moving design without much expenditure. At the other end of the scale is the production of full-length animated feature films which takes years and involves hundreds of artists at very high cost. For this very reason, a certain compromise is usually essential with mass audiences for universal acceptance of the film, and it explains perhaps why the design performance is often pushed into the background. Nevertheless, feature-length animated films such as "Animal Farm", "Yellow Submarine", "Fritz the Cat", "Lord of the Rings" and "Heavy Metal" may contain progressive and novel graphic design ideas.

Some advertising films in the cinemas could also reveal new conceptions in graphic design to attract audiences, especially since such productions could be milestones in the development of contemporary graphics. But the most conspicuous graphic design ideas usually come from experiments in three to ten minute films from countries like Yugoslavia, Poland, Hungary and Canada, where designers are not subjected to the obligation of immediate material pressures. In the meantime, also in the USA and Great Britain many enthusiastic designers devote their own money and time to the medium of film graphics, trying out new ideas. It would be unfair to ignore their efforts and achievements.

Due to its wide range of flexibility, film animation has become one of the major areas of graphic experimentation. Some critics maintain that the medium is the most dynamic form of visual invention today. Its capabilities of combining pictorial content with sound in time and space are certainly expressions of our contemporary existence. For the designer, film animation could also provide a new viewpoint: On the one hand, this medium is able to release him from being the middleman between the industrialist and the consumer public. On the other hand, as a communication artist between two major forces, it is the designer's function to sell the product to the consumer as quickly as possible. With the medium of film graphics, the designer is able to be completely free with the entire content of his material, without the influence of any other obligation. And then again, when he becomes a commercial artist, which is a task practically no designer can be relieved from today, he must bring an element of freshness, with visual ideas and striking effects into an assignment which no other medium than film graphics is able to provide.

"Under the Spell of Gambrinus", 1981.

Dirk Deparfe/B.

Super 8   16-mm

35-mm

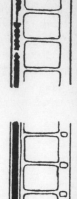

65-mm

1 *Comparative sizes of optical film: Super 8/16 mm/35 mm/65 mm.*
2 *Sound track on optical 35 mm and 16 mm film. 3 Magnetic Sound track.*

John Halas, Roger Manvell, 1970/GB.

Comparative sizes of a character have to be determined at the start of any production. ▷
Character from "Autobahn", 1979.

Design: Roger Mainwood/Production: Halas & Batchelor, Educational Film Centre/GB.

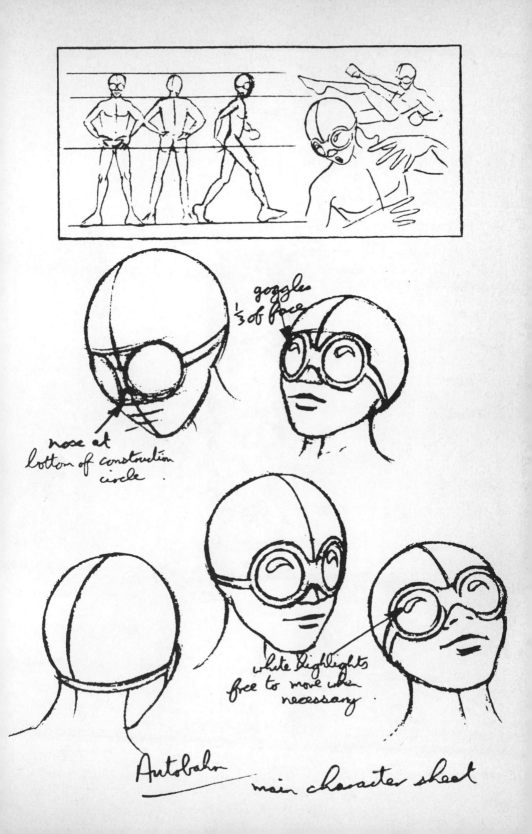

goggles
⅓ of face

nose at
bottom of construction
circle.

white highlights
free to move when
necessary

Autobahn   main character sheet

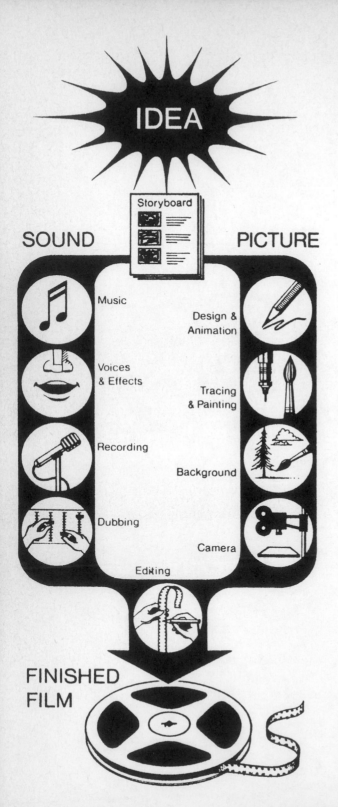

IDEA

Storyboard

SOUND   PICTURE

Music

Voices & Effects

Recording

Dubbing

Design & Animation

Tracing & Painting

Background

Camera

Editing

FINISHED FILM

Structure of production – from idea to finished film.

John Halas, 1976/GB.

2   3

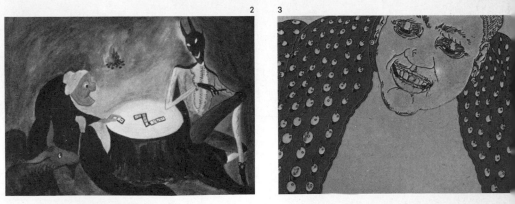

Close relationship between foreground figures and background provides a unity of graphic images.
1 "The Salamanna Grape", 2 "The Mask of the Devil", 3 "Dinner".

1 Manfredo Manfredi/I, 2 Kali Carlini/F, 3 Zlatko Bourek/YU.

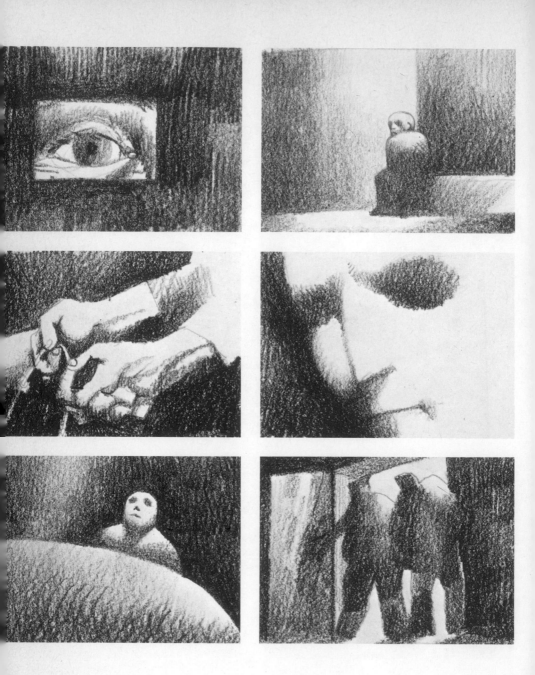

24

◁ Strong tonal rendering of light and
   shade achieves a dramatic effect.
   "Dedalo" (Labyrinth), 1978.

   Manfredo Manfredi, Cineteam/I.

Finger painting frame by frame under the
camera on glass retains the textures of
the painted surface. "The Street", 1976.

Caroline Leaf, National Film Board of
Canada.

A film made entirely from cut-outs.

Design: Frank Mouris, Frank Film, 1975/USA.

Puppet animation from Germany.
"Sweep Baby Sweep".

Miroslav Zahradnik, Südwestfunk
Baden-Baden/D.

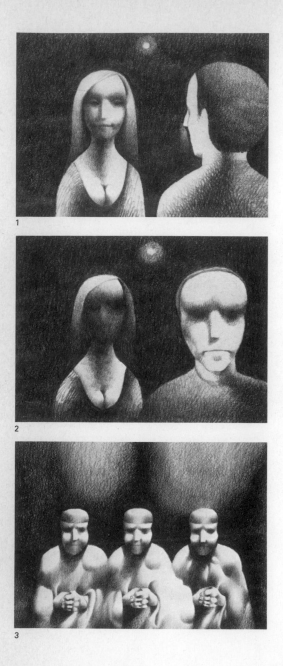

1–3 *"Dedalo" (Labyrinth),*
4 *"Ten for Survival".*

Manfredo Manfredi, Cineteam/I.

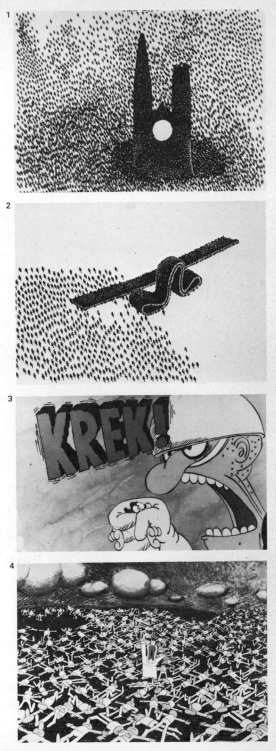

A highly dramatic use of black and white shapes.
1/2 "Perpetuo", 3 "The Enchanted Prince", 4 "Demagogue".

1/2 Joško Marušić, 3 Zlatko Pavliníc, 4 Radivoj Gvozdanović, YU.

Rich textural interpretation of Mozart's "Magic Flute" in an Italian style.
1–4 "The Magic Flute", 1977, 5/6 "Pulcinella", 1977.

Emanuele Luzzati, Giulio Gianini/I.

Tonal textures are made possible by the use of cut-outs.
1/3 "Antennae on Ice", 1978, 2 "A Taste of Happiness", 1976, 4 "Quod Libet", 1976, 5 "cube Mencube", 1976, 6 "Dinner", 1977.

1/3 R. Raamat/SU, 2 Niek Reus/NL, 4 Gerrit van Dijk/NL, 5 Gerrit van Dijk/NL, 6 Zlatko Bourek/YU.

1 *"Great", 1975,*
2 *"Queen", 1976.*

1 *Bob Godfrey Films/GB,*
2 *Gerrit van Dijk/NL.*

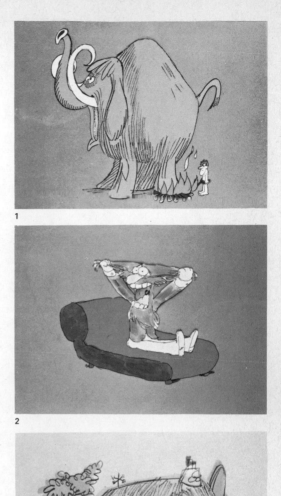

1

2

3

1/2 *"Making Music Together",*
3 *"Kitchen Think".*

1/2 *Geoff Dunbar, Jim Duffy, Produc-*
tion: Halas & Batchelor/GB f. Schering
Corporation/USA,
3 *Lee Mishkin, Production:*
Halas & Batchelor/GB f. The Gas Council/GB.

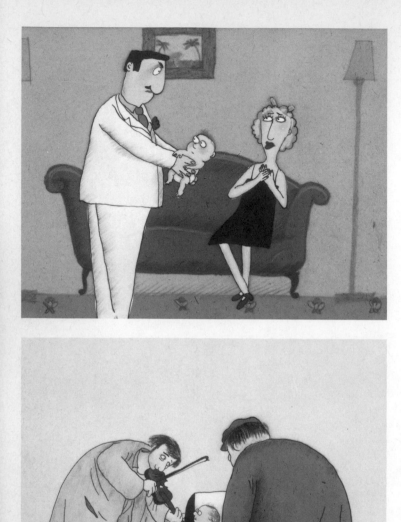

Humour in content and design is the key to the Oscar winning short film "Every Child", 1979, made for the UNICEF Italian Committee.

Derek Lamb/Eugene Fedorenko, National Film Board of Canada.

Classical visual art can be made to move.

Design: Pavao Stalter/Y.

Simple line drawings are being used in the film "Players", a satire on power politics, using the characters of Björn Borg and John McEnroe.

Production, Direction: John Halas, Assistant Direction, Design: Peter Sis/ GB, CS.

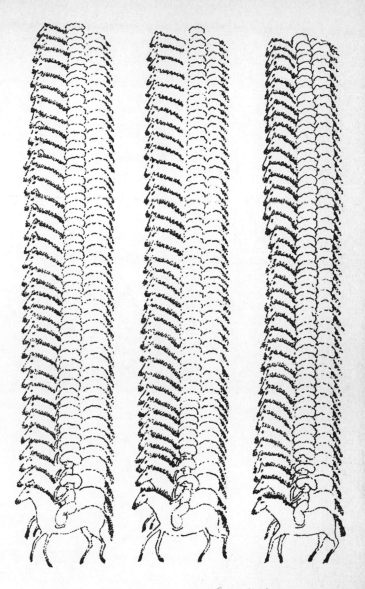

"Players", an Anglo-Czechoslovakian production.
Produced and directed by John Halas, Assistant Direction and
Design by Peter Sis.

37

"Panic", 1977.

Sandor Reisenbuckler, Pannonia Film/H.

1 Typical Russian traditions are maintained in the film by the talented team
of Ivanov-Vano and Juri Norstein.
2 Tallin Studio in Estonia, breaking away from old traditions with contemporary graphics.

1 Direction: Ivanov-Vano, Soyuz Multifilm/SU, 2 Direction: E. Tuganov, Tallin Studio/SU.

Wilhelm Busch comes to life through stop-motion animation.
1 "Smile Please", 2 "Johnny's Brave Descent".

1 Graham Ralph, 2 Brian Larkin (Halas & Batchelor for Polymedia).

40

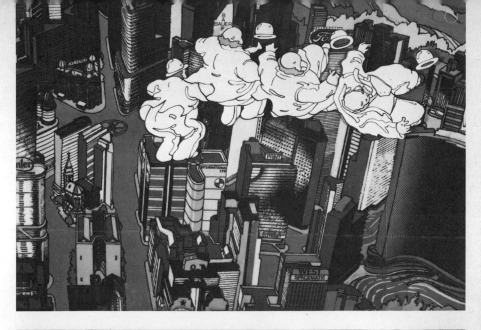

A contemporary graphic style is introduced for a film on Greed. "Hamm", 1978.

Istvan Bányai, Pannonia Film Studio/H.

This film, a science fiction tale produced in Chechoslovakia, is a feature length animated production. Three cartoonists, Topor, Ylipe and Folon have contributed to the making of the film's designs.

René Laloux/F.

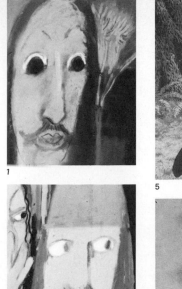

Animation with pastels under the camera.
1–4 "This is your Museum Speaking", 1979,
5 "Ludas Matyi", 1978, 6/7 "He, Tel", 1977.

1–4 Lynn Smith, National Film Board of Canada,
5 Marcel Jankovics, Atilla Dargay/H,
6/7 Peter Szoboszlay/H.

"Diary", 1972.

Nedeljko Dragić, Zagreb Film / YU.

Flexibility and a free flow of textural animation is evident in the film "Satiemania", 1978, by Zdenko Gasparović.

Zagreb Film / YU.

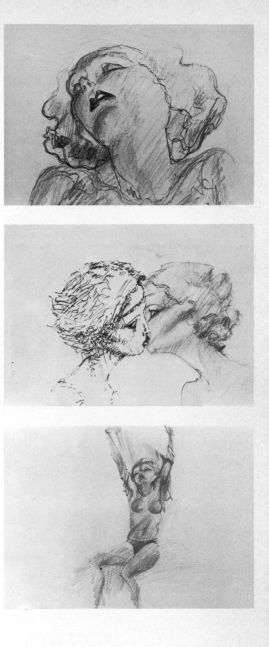

Humour in Character Design.
1/2 "Hoffnung Symphony Orchestra", 1965,
3 "Butterfly Ball", 1974.

1/2 Design: Alan Aldridge/GB,
Production: Halas & Batchelor/GB,
3 Design: Tom Bailley/GB,
Production: Halas & Batchelor/GB.

Breaking away from conventions ▷
by animating with audio-visual pencils.
1 "Anima", 1969,
2 "A Bogar" (The Bug), 1980.

1 Giselle Ansorge/CH,
2 Ferenc Rofusz/H.

1

2

1

2

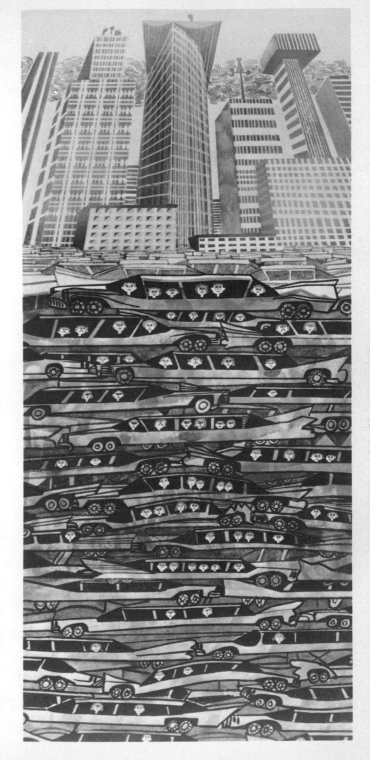

1 "Oh My Darling",
1977,
2 "Boom", 1979.

1 Borge Ring/NL,
2 Bretislav Pojar/CS.

Dramatic panning move-
ment used in the Academy
Award winning film "Auto-
mania 2000", 1963.

Direction: John Halas,
Halas & Batchelor/GB.

1 "Learning to Walk", 2 "Maxi Cat".

1 Borivoj Dovniković-Bordo, Zagreb/YU, 2 Zlatko Grgić, Zagreb Film/YU.

Three-dimensional stop-motion photography maintains the Czech tradition of puppetry.
1 "Apple Tree Girl", 1976, 2 "The Fox and the Hare", 1976, 3 "King of the Cats", 1979.

1 Bretislav Pojar/CS, 2 Juri Norstein/SU, 3 Pozena Mozisova/CS.

51

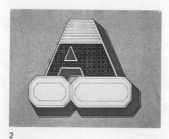

1

2

3

1 "Daphnis et Chloe", 1974,
2 "Mirror of Art", 1975, 3 "XYZ", 1975.

1 Peter Foldes, ORTF/F,
2 Pierre-Yves Pelletier, TV, CBC/CDN,
3 André Théroux, TV, CBC/CDN.

1 A film about the complex problems of ▷
environmental pollution for IBM Corporation.
"Of Men and Demons".
2 From an experimental film
by Halas & Batchelor. "Quartet".

1 Direction: John Hubley/USA,
2 Direction: Tony White/GB.

Imaginative animation with sand. "Sand Castle".

Co Hoedman, National Film Board of Canada.

*European Folk Tales. 1 "Cinderella Barber", 2 "Serpent's Tongue", 3 "Catalina and Catalin",
4 "The Trumpeter of Cracow", 5 "Halewyn", 6 "Dragon Snail".*

*1 Secondo Bignardi/I, 2 Aleksander Marks/YU, 3 Laurentiu Sirbu/BG,
4 Miroslaw Kijowitz/PL, 5 Raoul Servais/B, 6 Michel Clarence/B.*

"John Gilpin's Ride", 1951.

Design: Ronald Searle/GB, Production: Halas & Batchelor/GB.

1 "It Furthers One To Have Somewhere To Go", 1969, ▷
2 "The New Halas & Batchelor", 1970.

1 Design: Ginger Gibbons, Gillian Lacey/GB,
2 Design: Geoff Dunbar, Production: Halas & Batchelor/GB.

1

2

Bringing a new dimension into graphics animation with texturized figures.
"The Hedgehog and the Mist", 1976.

Juri Norstein/SU.

"Nutcracker Suite", 1975.

Boris Stepancev, Soyuz Multfilm/SU.

Alan Aldridge's graphic style adapted with full animation. "Butterfly Ball", 1974.

Design: Alan Aldridge, Halas & Batchelor/GB.

"Film, Film, Film", 1971.

Feodor Khitruk, Soyuz Multfilm/SU.

1–5 "Opens Wednesday", 1980, 6 "The Un-lucky Boy", 1978, 7 "The Leaves and the Roots", 1976.

1–5 Barrie Nelson/USA, 6 Jiri Brdecka/CS, 7 Leonid Nosirov, SU.

△ 1 "Bird and Worm", 1973, 2 "Lion's Share", 1974, 3 "Animalia", 1977, 4 "The Last Cartoon Man", 1974, 5 "My Friend the Hedgehog", 1976.

1 Zlatko Grgić, Zagreb Film/YU, 2 Ante Zaninovic, Zagreb Film/YU, 3 T. Hernadi, I. Majoros, Pannonia Film/H, 4 Jeffrey Hale, Derek Lamb/USA, 5 Jozsef Gemes, Pannonia Film/H.

1

2

3

4

5

6

7

1/2 "The Little Time Machine",
3/4 "Three Fats".

Valentina and Zinaida Brumberg, Soyuz
Multfilm/SU.

1/2 "Oh Fashion, Fashion", 3/4 "Gena The Crocodile", 5/6 "The Cyclist".

1/2 V. Bakhtadze, Gruziafilm/SU, 3/4 R. Kachanov, Soyuz Multifilm/SU,
5/6 Lev Atamanov, Soyuz Multifilm/SU.

◁ *Children's drawings brought to life. "Ten for Survival", 1979.* △ *"Optimist, Pessimist", 1974.*

Kati Macskassy/H (f. UNICEF).   *Zlatko Grgić, Zagreb Film/YU.*

1 "David", 2 "Smile", 3 "Claustro-phobia", 4 "Dojoji Temple", 5 "Union Gas" (Squirrel).

1 Paul Driessen/NL, 2 Pavel Prochazka/D, 3 Philippe Leclerc/F, 4 Kihachiro Kawamoto/J, 5 Mike Mills/CDN.

1 "Whale Songs", 2 "Alternativa", 3 "Bubblicious", 4 "Instant Sex", 5 "The Tale of Tales", ▷
6 "Nocturna Artificialia", 7 "Les 3 Inventeurs", 8 "Alouette".

1 Mary Beams/USA, 2 Roumen Petkov/BG, 3 Susan Rubin/USA, 4 Bob Godfrey/GB, 5 Juri Norstein/SU, 6 The Brother Quay/GB, 7 Michel Ocelot/F, 8 Michèle Panzé/CDN.

1

2

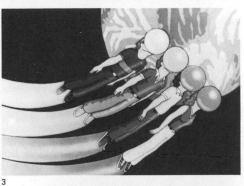

3

4

5

6

7

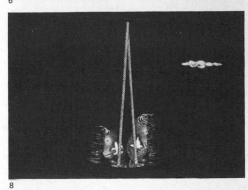

8

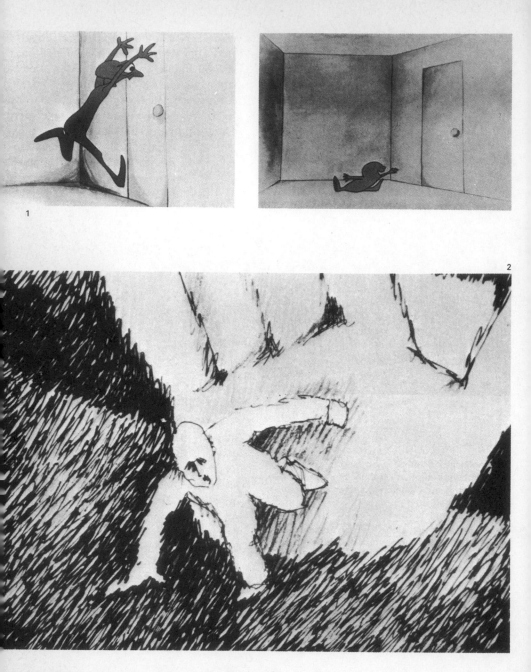

1/2 "Room and Board", 1974, 3 "Tyranny", 1974.

1/2 Randy Cartwright/USA, 3 Philippe Fausten/F.

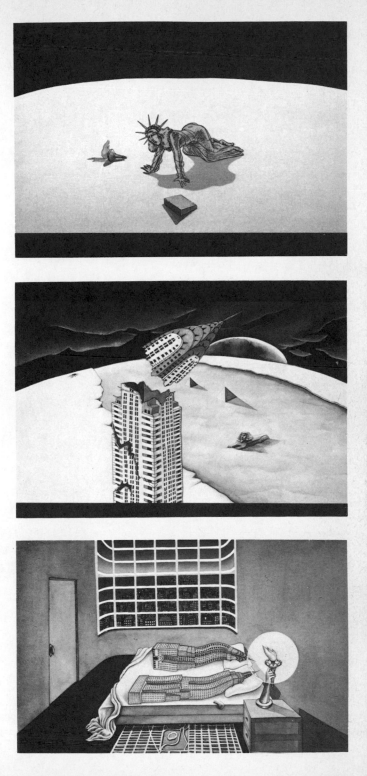

"Flagrant Delit", 1979.

Jean Pierre Jacquet/F.

"Les Corbeaux", 1967.

Ernest and Giselle Ansorge/CH.

1 "Desert", 1981,
2 "Skyscraper", 1981,
3 "After Beardsley", 1981.

1 José Xavier/F,
2 Joško Marušić,
Zagreb Film/YU,
3 Chris James/GB.

Spacial movement using coloured textures.
"The Oriental Nightfish", 1979.

Ian Emes/GB.

1 *"The Principles of Flying"*, 2 *"Potpourri"*.

1 *Animation: Don Bluth/USA*, 2 *Production: Les Kaluza/USA.*

1 "Simple Simon", 2 "Alphabet", 3 "The Long Drawn Out Trip".

1 Jeffrey Hale f. »Sesame Street«/USA, 2 Holly Zapp/USA, 3 Gerald Scarfe/USA.

TV Graphics

The Bible comes alive in strong graphic style. "Noah's Ark", 1978.

Halas & Batchelor, Dino Katopoulis/GB, CDN.

"Everything for Nothing".

Hubert Tison

The meaning of TV graphics should be divided into two different contexts. First, productions primarily designed for the TV screen. Second, productions which can only be carried out by equipment belonging to television technology.

In the first category, one refers to simplified films with smaller budgets than those for cinema films which, as a consequence of higher budgets, enjoy greater sophistication and are visually richer. In the case of small television screens economies can be introduced without detriment to the graphic content. This is especially true of children's television entertainment.

This approach, however, does not apply to television advertising which is not economically restricted and where production values very likely play an essential part in achieving the objective – persuasion. However, in the context of this book, I am attempting to deal with areas of activity produced for television by designers working primarily in this specialized field.

Considering the totality of visual communication, very few industries have grown in such a phenomenal way as television. With over 120 countries relaying regular services, some from early morning to late at night, some programmes attracting 20 million viewers, or up to 400 million if the relay is international during sports events, for example, here is a new opportunity for the graphic designer to provide creativity and ideas within the framework of visual communication.

Television is a field where the demand for graphic presentation on a year-to-year basis is rapidly expanding. As mechanisation is developing it undergoes a continuous change. It is a field where the services of the graphic designer need not be confined to presentation only. His involvement in programme planning and content could also be significant, especially in achieving graphic unity.

The range of design performance has progressed rapidly from a modest start when only a typographic title presentation was required. Today, beyond titles and credits, programme promotion, education conceived through visual diagrams, inserts, background effects, children's entertainment, announcements of a great variety including weather reports, and stage designs, all make up the range of assignments.

Three factors have to be realised in relationship with TV graphics:

1. The designer is a member of a team.
2. The performance is purely in terms of its technology.
3. The deadlines are determined by transmission dates demanding what one may term "instant" graphics.

The graphic designer is a member of a tightly organised team headed by a TV producer and director, and there is a need for close internal communication between all members. Apart from his/her skill, the design performance must be carried out in terms of television equipment which can vary from station to station and from country to country. The designer's understanding of the fundamentals of what is or what is not possible in electronic vision, recording and transmission is vital. These would include considerations given not only to such basic factors as typographic legibility on the TV tube with an aspect ratio of 4:3, but also to what would appear on the flickering surface of the tube, which contains only a limited number of reference points within which the final design presentation will take place. One should never forget that while the cathode ray tube, which serves as the terminal for the computer as a rule, has a high resolution of 1025×1025 reference point, the domestic TV set may contain only 405, 525, 625 or 819 lines (according to the different countries) which are indeed limiting factors to definition and subtle design. There is a danger of flickering and strobing when one uses horizontal and vertical lines or patterns unless, of course, one purposely incorporates these incidental happenings as visual effects with video techniques. Another limiting factor is the high light intensity which produces blinding glare on the surface of the tube.

There are basic differences between monochrome and colour systems. In Western Europe 40% receive their programmes in black and white (in the USA 90% have colour), so from the start designers are obliged to consider both systems. The measure is in the form of gray scale. While a colour system can distinguish twenty different grays, a black and white system can only cope with ten shades. A further limitation arises in the possibility of distortion of tones on a monochrome receiver. Dark colours such as purple, deep blue and green quite easily fall off and appear pure black. On the other hand, light blue, yellow and pink can come out not only the same light gray shade but if painted too light, they can become white. These are the reasons why sophisticated design styles should be avoided and, if time allows, tests should be made before TV camera relays.

The problems of tone, colour, shade and composition also apply to set designing, costume, fabric, furniture and interior designs on television. However, design limitations may be compensated for by the video output of the TV camera, achieved by the electronic processing of the signals which are capable of producing some highly interesting graphics. These usually involve superimposing the video output from one camera over another, combining lettering and drawings with live images, creating special effects and abstract patterns, as well as synthesizing colour lines and varying them within the gray scale. One most definitely has to work with an electronic engineer familiar with the capabilities of a colour synthesizer (colour box) who, under the guidance of the designer, can operate the three primary colours from the monochrome scale and manipulate these for a carefully worked out visual effect.

It is not unusual that an emergency arises or that extra credits or announcements are required in the morning for the evening performance. At such high speed only an experienced designer can deliver the goods even if the latest computer printout systems are employed. In such cases there is little time for inspiration but there is the need for a knowledge of typography and a sense of layout, in order to maintain a high quality and a professional standard of design. As a rule, the programmes are pre-planned, if not years or months ahead (like the production of a film) at least weeks ahead, which provides an opportunity for the designer to contribute his skill and talent to the overall content of a programme. The cooperation of an enlightened producer who understands the potential of TV graphics as well as its range of techniques, and the electrical engineer who can carry out the ideas in terms of machine intelligence and have sympathy for them, are essential to make up a good team.

Beyond the basic design discipline lies the necessity for the TV designer to absorb a new language. The capacity of TV cameras, TV receivers, the sensitivity of frequency and scanning systems, caption scanners, tonal structures of television images, camera inlays, back and front projection, video playbacks and audio signals are concepts which belong to the vocabulary of everyday operation.

Original use of film material for a ▷ programme title.

Süddeutscher Rundfunk, 1974/D.

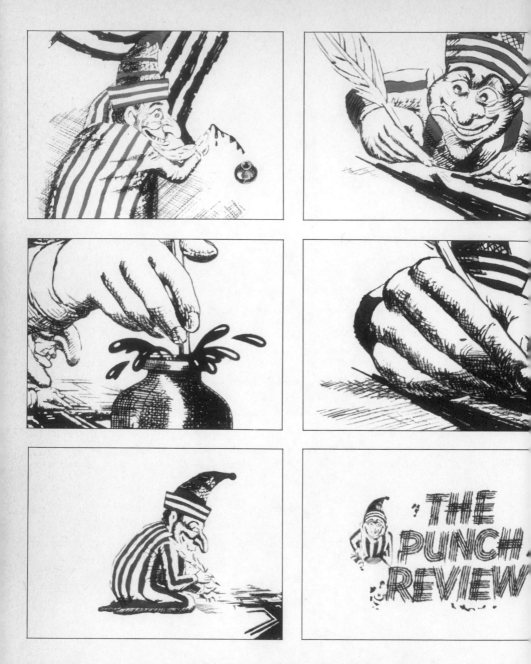

Title designs and programme announcements are the busiest area for the TV graphic designer. The opportunity for visual humour and graphic invention is boundless.

Punch Review, Stefan Petrowski, BBC London, 1976/GB.

André Théroux's style of using bold outlines is admirably suited to the medium of television.

André Théroux, CBC Montreal/CDN.

Children's entertainment TV film, with inspired graphic design by Frédéric Back. "Everything for Nothing", 1978.

Frédéric Back, CBC Montreal/CDN.

Children's TV programme for CBC. "The Tortoise and the Hare", 1979.

Graeme Ross, CBC, Montreal/CDN.

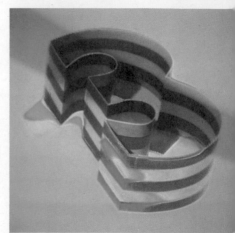

Three-dimensional paper cut-outs are utilised by Rob van de Berg for Dutch Television.

Rob van de Berg, KRO TV, 1974/NL.

Programme announcements with a strong graphic impact.

1 André Théroux, CBC, Montreal, 1975/CDN, 2 Daniel Mery, CBC, Montreal, 1975/CDN.

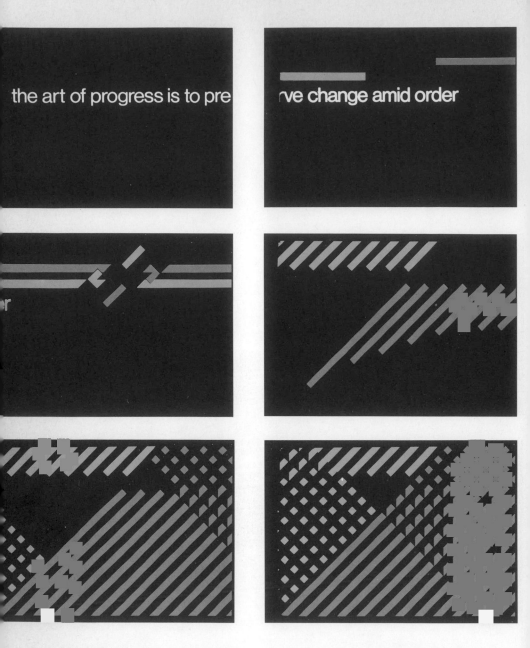

the art of progress is to pre | rve change amid order

Richard Greenberg's motion graphics have the combined quality of good design and imaginative visual solutions to a problem and are always carried through with up-to-date technology.

Richard Greenberg (f. Container Corporation of America, 1978), New York/USA.

Sequence for a TV announcement for the Container Corporation of America.

Design: Richard Greenberg/Production: R/R Greenberg Associates, New York, 1978/USA.

Title for Programme Previews.

Erich Sokol, 1974/AUS.

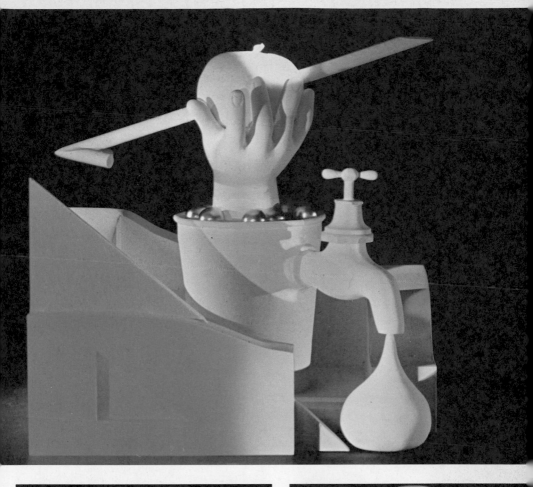

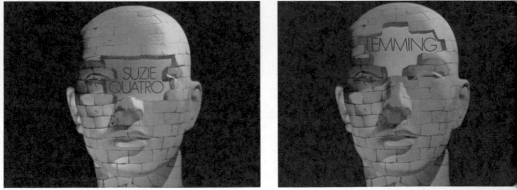

Effective use of moving coloured lights on three-dimensional objects for the presentation of credits.
"Coloured Lights", 1975.

Frans Schupp, AVRO TV/NL.

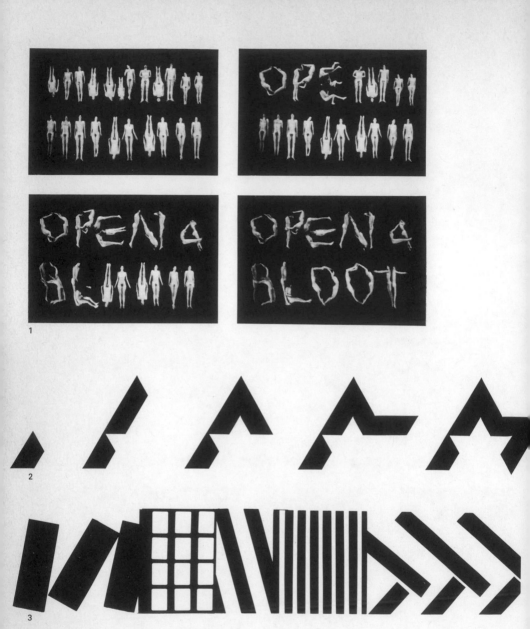

1 Shapes, forms and lettering are combined to project the content of a TV programme.
2/3 Modern abstract graphics are utilised in movement to achieve a strong visual impression.

1 Hans de Cocq, NOS TV, 1975/NL, 2 Stuart Ash, CBC, Montreal, 1975/CDN,
3 Jules Engel, 1974/USA.

Simple graphic lines are particularly effective on the small television screen. "The Cage", 1978.

Roger Mainwood, Royal College of Art, London/GB.

meeting with
Samuel Beckett

meeting with
Pablo Neruda

meeting with
Murray Gell-Mann

Titles for a TV series on Nobel prize winners.

Christian Devrient, Sveriges Radio, 1975/S.

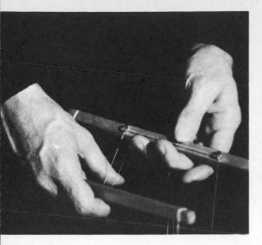

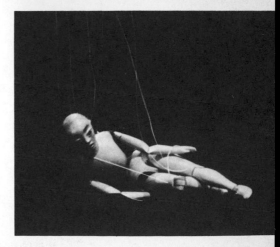

Title for a drama programme.
"Maria Marten", 1980.

Liz Friedmann, BBC TV/GB.

EVERYMAN

*A highly original solution for an introductory
title for a documentary programme about social   △ ▷
problems of the entire human race.*

Stewart Austin, BBC TV, 1980/GB.

The opening title for the "Max and Moritz" (1978) television series for ZDF.

Direction: John Halas, Production: Halas & Batchelor/GB and Polymedia/D.

Sequences from "Max and Moritz" (1978), TV Series based on Wilhelm Busch's classic characters.

Direction: John Halas, Production: Halas & Batchelor/GB and Polymedia/D.

TV Commercial. "Desserta", 1978. △

Production: Halas & Batchelor f. J. Walter Thompson/GB.

◁ *A sequence showing a somersault, from the "Max and Moritz" TV Series (1978).*

Direction: John Halas, Production: Halas & Batchelor/GB and Polymedia/D.

TV Commercial for Michelin Tyres, Paris.

Production: Halas & Batchelor, 1973/GB.

Video Graphics

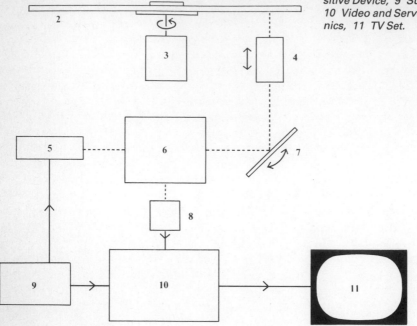

1 Video disc player, 2 Record, 3 Motor, 4 Objective, 5 Laser, 6 Optics, 7 Mirror, 8 Light-sensitive Device, 9 Supply, 10 Video and Servo Electronics, 11 TV Set.

Video graphics is a term denoting a medium-adapted type of graphics specially designed to meet the requirements of line scanning and contrasts on the TV screen. For this purpose the graphic designer must adapt the strength of the contours, the colours etc., and provide for electronic effects, which can be integrated immediately in the TV studio. Such effects are solarisation (reversal of pictures, abstraction, intensification of colour), deliberate colouring, negative effects, or the "blue box" process (masking).

Another potential for electronic visual effects is with video tape recording and its capability of visual feedback by arranging the cameras in such a way that they should mirror back their own amplified output. Through a series of amplifications the vision can then be infinitely bounced

back like a picture in opposite pairs of mirrors. A further application of electronic visual feedback is to create sound structures parallel with image structures out of the electronic impulses. The combination of video and tape recorders can provide sound impulses in real time comparable to an orchestra in a live concert. Just as the images, the sound can be stored and mixed at a later date. With this approach, for instance, F. Moormann Jr., of the Southern Illinois University, USA, has constructed a video system combining visuals with synthesized sound in space which he entitled "Video Space".

"Video freakery" is a term used to describe the creation of incidental effects with the trick mixer. By increasing the voltage output through the recording it is possible to distort a real image like a live face and achieve soft forms and diffuse outlines. Furthermore, the image can be improved by passing through a second effect (chroma-key or colour separation overlay) adding several layers of colour to it. This combination will lead to surprisingly sophisticated graphic effects.

Until now most results have been achieved by wipe generators, chroma-key units and colour generators, all of which are standard video graphic equipment in a TV studio. Lately, specially designed video colour synthesizer equipment has been introduced, such as the "Spectre", which is able to combine the separate units into one group. This system has a high perceptual impact and gives freedom to combine shapes and colours specifically and also in a general way. It is basically a digital signal matrix-board. With this highly sophisticated machine the videographic designer can manipulate functions manually through the eight control inputs to achieve his visual effects. The moving (or static) colour images are assembled on a normal 625 PAL video format. The controls of the eight shape generators determine the horizontal and vertical positions, the horizontal and vertical zooms, and the size of circles. Not all of these control inputs need be applied to every shape. Some shapes, like the circle, are only altered by the horizontal and vertical position and by circle size.

At first sight, these control panels as well as the output columns (consisting of a digital signal matrix and an analog control matrix) look absolutely incomprehensible to the designer who is accustomed to creating his forms manually. This electronic visual effects generator, which is arranged with the addition of visual symbols, makes design vocabulary almost limitless. At this stage however, video graphics still require an optical camera feedback and the recycling transformation from optical to electronic images and vice versa, make the system interdependent to a very great extent.

There are endless variations in the potential of visual manipulation with TV and video and it is only in its first phase of development. Yet its application is already wide, ranging from audio-visual educational technology in modern aircraft training, to extreme abstract art with complex electronically generated geometric patterns, and the creation of textile and wallpaper designs. In the middle range lies the day-to-day application of TV graphics carried out by resident graphic designers in not less than eighty countries within the compounds of well over a hundred television studios and several thousand research establishments and universities throughout the world.

Video graphics can also play an important role in large-scale feature films where the production of normal optical special effects techniques cannot achieve the desired visual effects. However, both the equipment necessary (e.g. the "Anspex VR 1200 Quadruplex" machine) as well as the engineering skills needed to manipulate it, are well beyond the scope of the practising graphic designer, especially in view of the expenditure.

There is no doubt that increasing use is being made of video graphic techniques in visual communication, particularly in experimental arts. By starting to practise with the simpler U-Matic machine, designers could eventually gain the experience needed to operate the normal broadcast standard of two-inch magnetic tape.

It is inevitable that, as television stations gradually transmit from video tape rather than from optical film, video technology will become more important. In the meantime, if a designer and producer wish to convert work created through video tape, there are transfer systems to 35 and 16 mm optical film without substantial loss of quality.

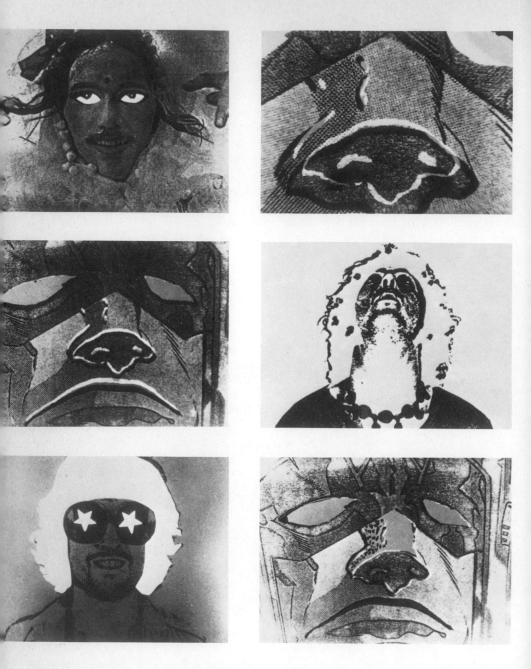

Video and optical effects combined. "Xerography", 1972.

Direction: Geoff Dunbar, Production: Halas & Batchelor/GB.

Monochrome off-screen reproductions of colour originals, being Spectre-processed versions mainly of the monochrome photograph top left.

Design: Richard Monkhouse, William Kentish, 1976/GB.

One of the first uses of videographics: the BBC TV Programme "Doctor Who" (1975).

Bernard Lodge, BBC London/GB.

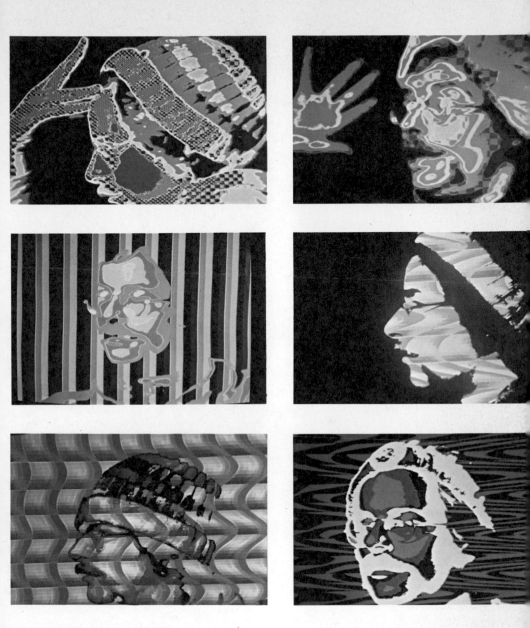

Camera feedback forms an essential part of video graphics, which may very well open up a new era for visual arts.

Design/Program: Richard Monkhouse, 1976/GB, Photos/Graphics: William Kentish, 1976/GB.

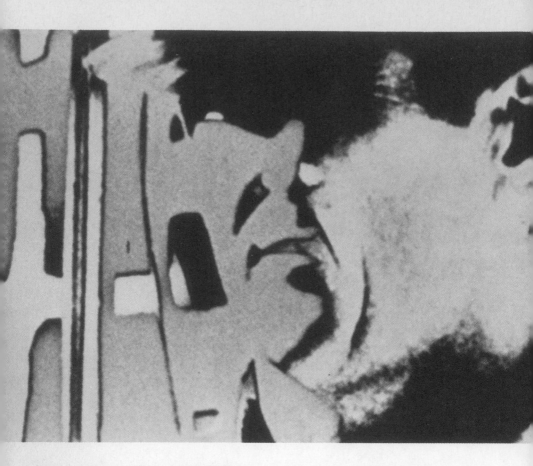

Video Modification. "Solarisation", 1975.

Design: Morton u. Mildred Goldscholl/USA.

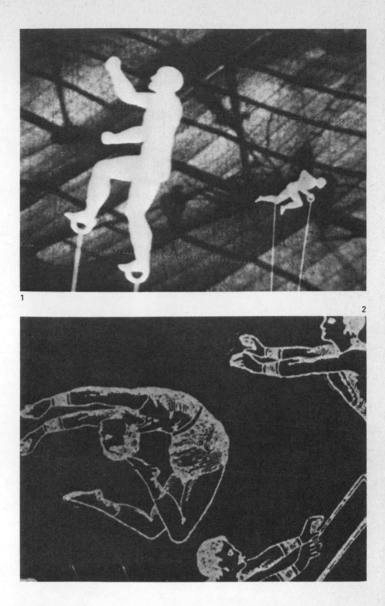

Video Modifications designed by Morton/Mildred Goldscholl:
1 with stencils, 2 with electronic "pencil" (1975).

Goldscholl Design Associates/USA.

Richard Monkhouse, leading pioneer of video graphics technology, assisted in designing the EMS Spectre Video Synthesizer.

Design/Program: Richard Monkhouse, 1976/GB, Photos /Graphics: William Kentish, 1976/GB.

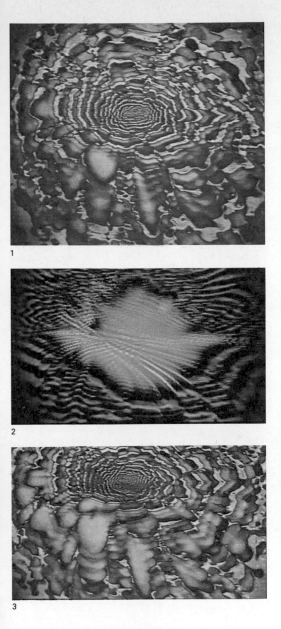

1

2

3

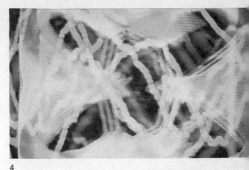

4

5

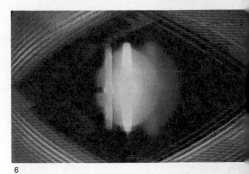

6

*The production of video graphics through
video synthesisers is claimed to be the
ultimate in pictorial art.*

*1–3 Peter Donebaur, 1975/GB,
4–7 Doron Abrahami, 1975/GB.*

7

»Earthkeeping«, 1976.

Direction: Mildred Goldscholl, Animation: Paul Jessel/USA.

*Video Modifications designed by Morton/Mildred Goldscholl:
1 with stencils, 2 with electronic "pencil" (1975).*

Goldscholl Design Associates/USA.

1

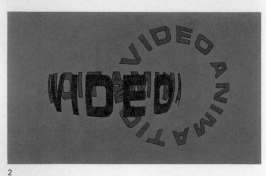

2

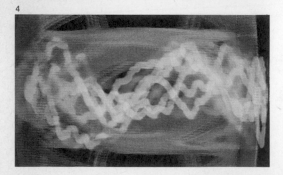

3

4

1/2 Computer Graphics and Title
produced at Imperial College of
Science and Technology, London.
3/4 Abstract film produced by
electronic modulator at
Royal College of Art, London.

1/2 Stan Hayward, Tony Diment,
1975/GB,
3/4 Doron Abrahami, 1975/GB.

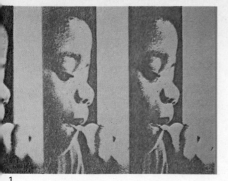

1

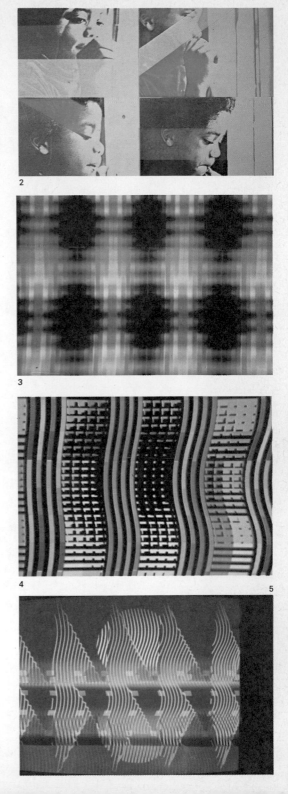

2

3

4

5

1/2 Stills from "Hello", using copy-motion technique.
3–5 Geometric patterns produced with X-Y Generators, using video feedback to produce colour shifts.

1/2 Eduardo Darino, 1976, New York/USA.
3–5 Richard Monkhouse, 1976/GB.

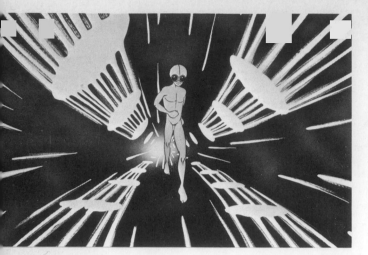

"Autobahn" is a forerun- ▷
ner in specially created
productions for the newly
emerging video-disc
home market.

Design:
Roger Mainwood,
Production and
Direction: John Halas,
1979/GB.

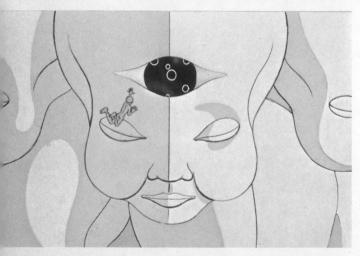

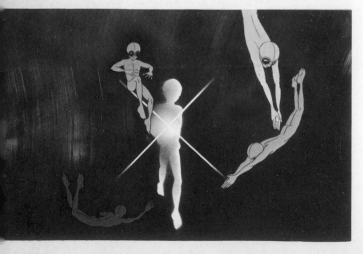

"Autobahn", a combined
computer/manual pro-
duction based on the rock
music of the group
"Kraftwerk".

Design:
Roger Mainwood,
Production and
Direction: John Halas,
1979/GB.

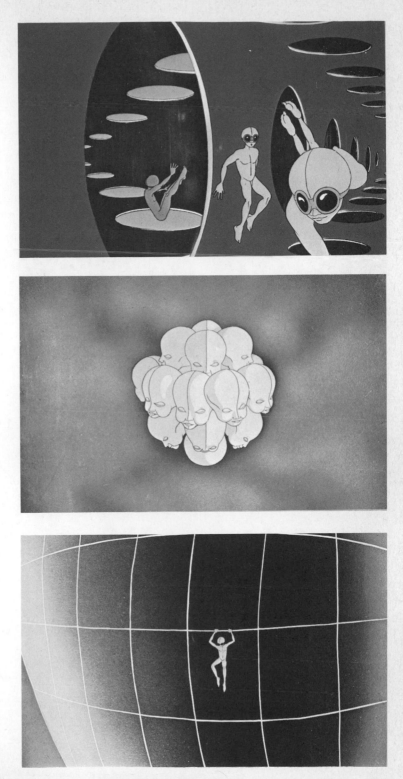

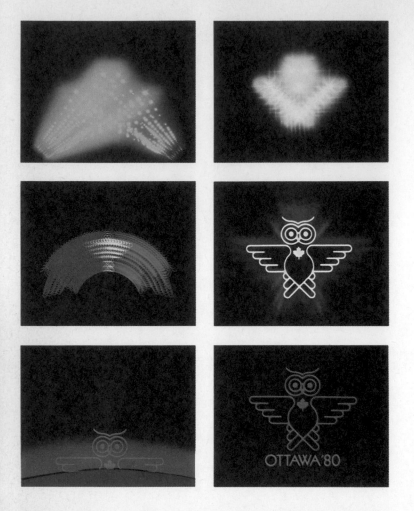

Programme opening for Ottawa Film Festival, by combined computer and video graphics.

Art Direction: George Iro, Design: Gerard Bueche, Production: CBC, Toronto, 1980/CDN.

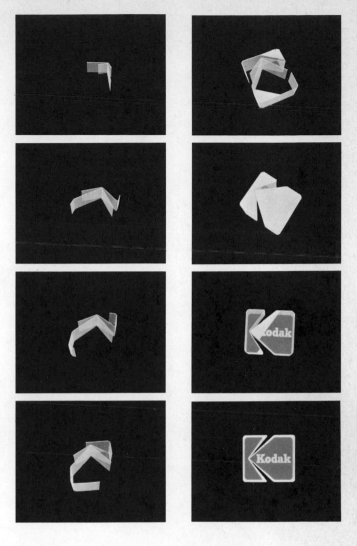

Station Logo for JWT, New York by Luminetics.

Art Direction: Robert Abel, Design: Con Pederson, 1976/USA.

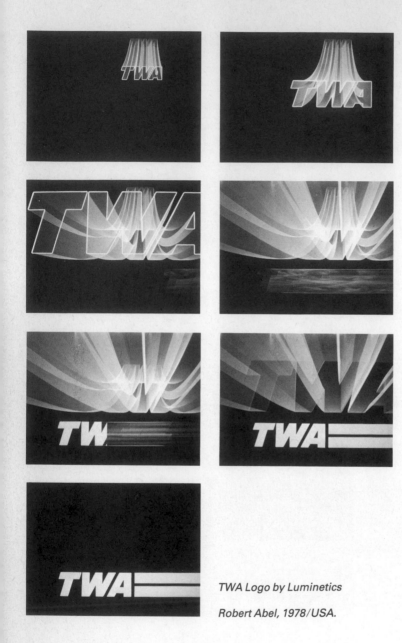

TWA Logo by Luminetics

Robert Abel, 1978/USA.

"Experienced Consumer", programme title for Radio Canada. ▷

Design: Paul Lévesque, 1978/CDN.

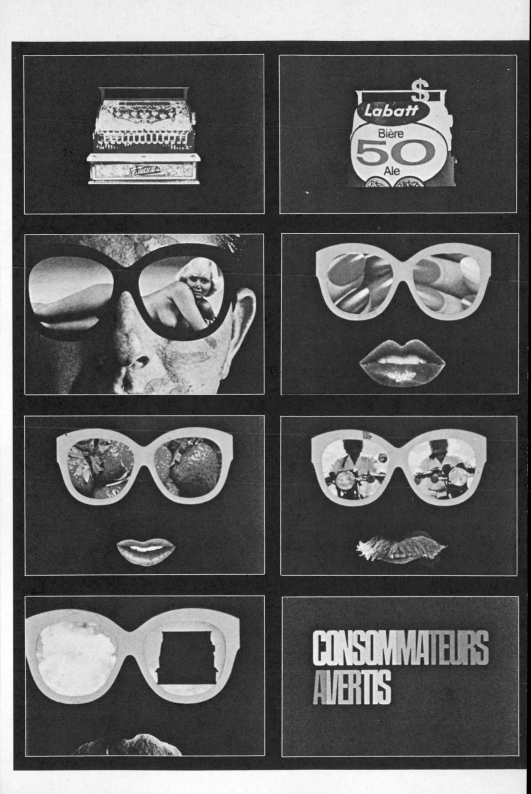

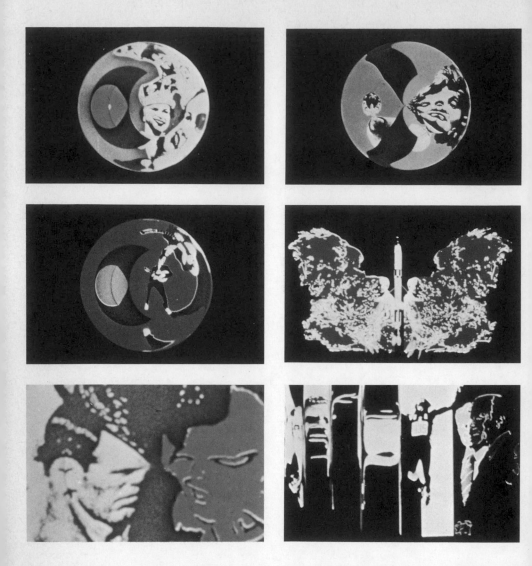

From a programme celebrating the 25th anniversary of Canadian TV. "25 Years of Information", 1979.

André Théroux, Radio Canada, Montreal/CDN.

"Forum", programme title for Radio Canada. ▷

Art Direction: Hubert Tison, Design: François Dallaire, 1979/CDN.

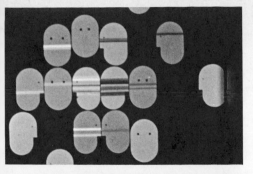
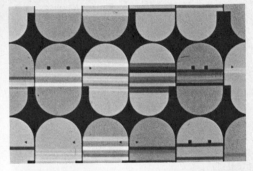
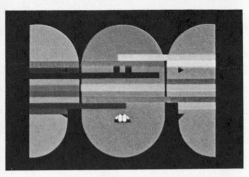

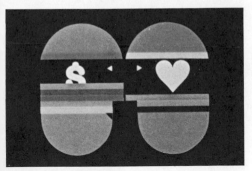
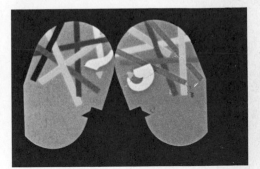
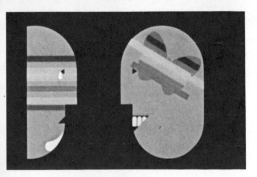

Computer Graphics

The motivation for the use of machines to create moving graphic images is on two levels. First economic, second creative. On the question of economics, designers and film makers have searched for a long time to economise on human labour by delegating to certain mechanical processes the labour-consuming phases of hand-drawing which are required for an animated film. The computer has been adopted and utilised to achieve this objective successfully today, as was the electrical oscillator some years ago.

A sharp distinction must be made here in order not to confuse the various equipment used in electronic and video markets. Some, like the computer, can be put to use as an automatic drawing instrument and a device to produce the actual drawings and others, like TV and video cameras, are purely recording machines on magnetic tapes. It is, however, possible to utilise some magnetic tapes for the multiplication of images and thus achieve substantial labour savings. But it is the computer-generated graphics which are capable of causing an economic revolution in the field of mechanically reproduced images. This field embraces, not only many visually based industries such as architecture, the film industry, cartography and aerospace research but also the whole field of education and science.

Apart from savings of millions in human labour, computer-generated designs can be put to use in certain areas where visual references did not exist such as in predicting the behaviour of the elements thousands of years in the future and calculating what may have occurred millions of years in the past, as well as on a more practical level of visual analysis of car accidents and aeroplane behaviour against air resistance. The actual value of graphic images as designs of quality in their own right is purely incidental. Many scientific research projects have produced high quality graphics as a by-product of the computer. The University of Syracuse's galaxy formation project, showing 50,000 stars ascending into the galaxy in three minutes of film when it would have actually taken 2,000 million years in real time, is a case in point.

Apart from such remarkable achievements in the field of science, computer technology has developed into the most significant design tool of our decade. Some of the latest evidence of this is seen in the "Simulation of the Voyager Flight to Jupiter and Saturn" by Dr James Blinn of NASA. The simulation of aeroplane cockpits in pilot training and the development of prototypes both by Boeing in the USA and by Messerschmitt-Bölkow-Blohm, Dynamics Division in Munich, are further examples of the computer's capabilities.

Computer-generated and computer-assisted animation hit both the cinema and television screens in the early 1980's and now several systems are at the disposal of visualisers. The interactive contact between designer, artist and programmer has become easier to the benefit of all. Some of the systems in digital and analog types are at the stage where, by the turn of a knob, the designer can produce the graphic output of the computer in real time.

There has been substantial progress in modelling and display programmes by the illusion of three dimensions. Characters, machines and buildings can be created in colour, as well as geometric shapes like spheres, cylinders, cones and polygons and can be levitated weightlessly in space either in a realistic sense or in the form of imaginative fantasy. The creation of such synthetic movement was initiated by the New York Institute of Technology, and the work is continued on parallel lines in Hollywood by Lucasfilm of San Rafael, California. This specially formed unit for the exploitation of computer real time simulation systems has already been made good use of in the feature films "Star Wars" and "The Empire Strikes Back".

It would be out of context within the scope of this book to list all the areas of application for computer graphics, but one cannot pass over such achievements as those made in design engineering, manufacture, architecture, printing and particularly in typography as it is applied for television. Within the resolution of the PAL 625 line system (used both in Germany and Great Britain) the problems of legibility, clarity of vision, aesthetic spacing and spread, are constant headaches. The development of laser-scanned computer-controlled-typesetting with a prospect of interpolating alphabets at lower resolution for the TV medium is highly welcome. So is the improvement in the final reproductive quality and the storage facilities for recalling some types and designs.

From the time of Leonardo da Vinci until the end of the 18th century, Science and Art were much closer together than today. They separated out with greater specialization in all branches of science. Such a separation is dangerous and the resulting isolation has become one of the major problems in a contemporary society which requires study and action for further advances in science and technology and in the arts.

At present the initiative of computer graphics lies with the scientists who originated the visual aspect of the computer and who have greater access to the computer than the artists. It is clear that what is required is the computer-trained graphic designer/programmer who will be able to sit at the console and immediately see the programme on the face of the display tube and make changes instantly. This entails the learning of programme languages. New computer languages are being developed and designers no longer need to be expert mathematicians. Two hours of coaching would enable most designers to communicate instructions to the computer. The discovery of new dimensions, easy manipulation of space, depth of motion and random creative combinations will open up at the fingertips of the graphic designer. With these experiments new aesthetic experiences will be obtained and an era of closer co-operation and better understanding between graphics and science will begin.

The following sketch is one form of computer-generated animation which is capable of manipulating graphic images to produce moving pictures from the cathode ray tube. Other forms exist whereby input of the images generates the graphics from the circuits alone.

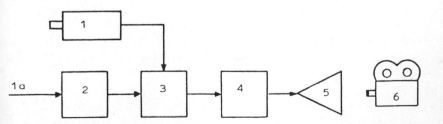

1 Pattern Scanner, 1a Instrucions, 2 Control Panel, 3 Analog Computer, 4 Display Hardware, 5 Display Tube, 6 24fps Camera

Raster Graphics Symbol

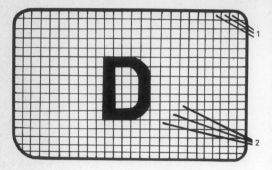

1 Computer Memory Adress, 2 Pixels

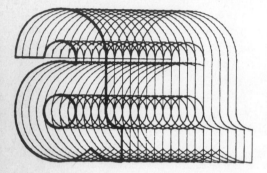

*Computer-generated title design for the book
"What Is A Computer?"
by John Halas/GB.*

A highly simplified description of computer graphics is:

1. Raster graphics which are produced by dividing the picture into small raster areas or picture elements, called "pixels" which contain a number of specific advantages such as memory retention, brightness and colour control; all of which can be maintained in each pixel for every single frame of a project. Each picture area or "grid" may contain thousands of pixels, each containing specific numerical values. Therefore, in this raster graphics digital method, each pixel is subjected to a predetermined and calculated value which can be defined with great precision.

2. Vector graphics are based on the Cartesian coordinate system. This method does not provide similar storage capacity to that of raster graphics. Shading and colours are added later in the post-production period. A combined use of both is possible and is at present being developed. However, the raster graphics system is favoured due to its greater flexibility.

*Bob Abel, Hollywood, who developed the
"Luminetics" System, is a highly creative art
director making a strong impact with modern
technology (1976).*

«LUMINETICS»

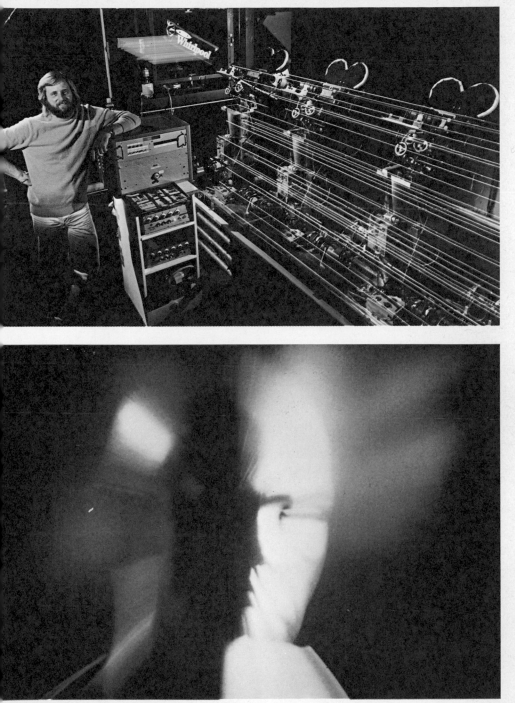

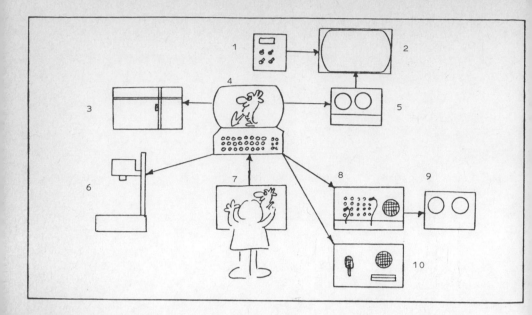

A system of computer animation including the synchronisation of sound track (with kind permission of Stan Hayward). 1 Colour and Pattern Generator, 2 Video Display, 3 Graph Plotter, 4 Computer and Display, 5 Video Recorder, 6 Rostrum, 7 Digitiser, 8 Sound Synthesizer, 9 Sound Recorder, 10 Voice Analyser/Editor.

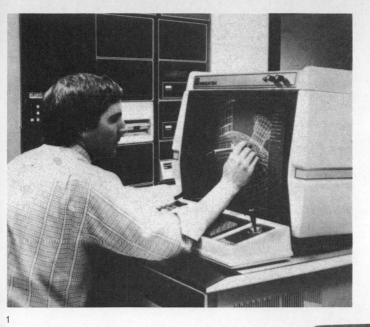

1 Simulation: Robert Abel, 1977, Holly-
wood/USA. 2 Three-dimensional
modelling and interpolation. Design: Eric
Brown, Miles Laboratories, 1977/USA.

2

Three-dimensional translation of a logo-type into motion, by the "Luminetics" System.

RCA Logo f. J. Walter Thompson, New York. Art Direction: Robert Abel, Ken Duskin, Design: Robert Abel, Dave Stewart, 1976/USA.

Early application involved the use of a so-called flying spot scanner. A digital signal contained the picture information for computer processing.

Lillian F. Schwartz, Charles B. Rubinstein, 1970/USA.

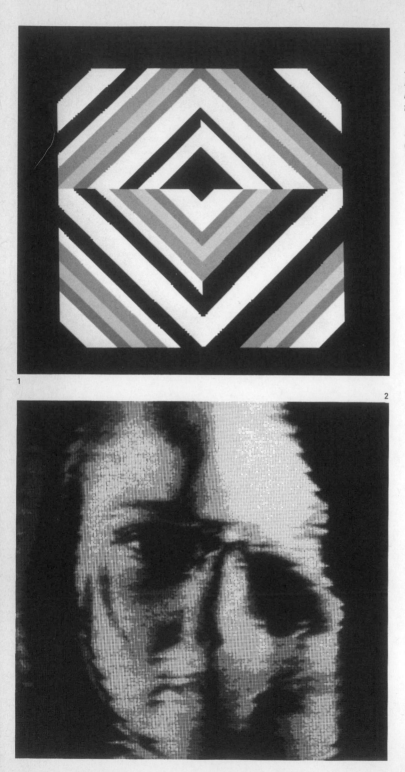

1 Abstract image
wholly generated by
the computer.
2 Two faces are com-
bined into one by mov-
ing parts of one to
the other.

Lillian F. Schwartz,
Charles B. Rubinstein,
1971/USA.

1

2

1 Computerized radar. A
motion in 360° from "Con-
tact", produced by Educa-
tional Film Centre for Com-
pagnie Générale d'Electri-
cité/F. 2 Building con-
struction analysed by the
computer to show heat/
energy conversion.

1 Direction: John Halas,
Joy Batchelor, 1973/GB,
2 Computergraphics:
Brian Borthwick,
John Halas, 1977/GB.

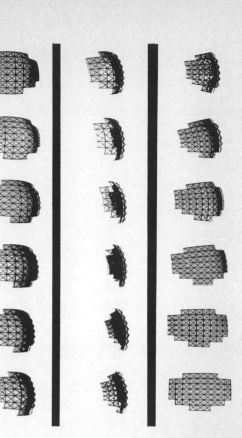

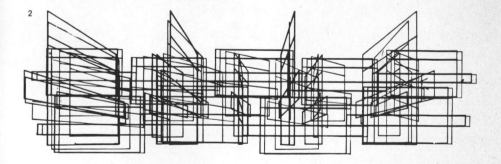

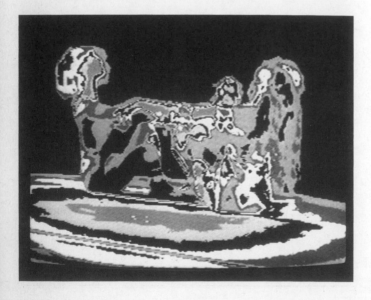

An essential aspect of computer technology is the exploration of media in the form of abstract art, breaking away from established traditions. Lillian F. Schwartz has been a pioneer of computer graphics as art during the last decade.

Lillian F. Schwartz, 1976/USA.

The simulation of aircraft landing and aerodynamics is an essential practice in the aircraft construction industry. The building of Concorde benefited from this, as did Boeing in the USA and Messerschmitt in Germany.

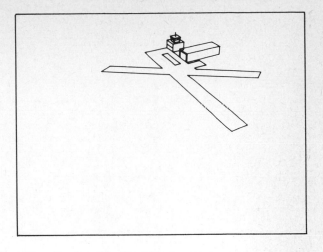

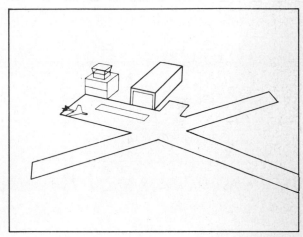

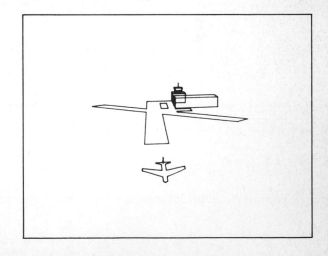

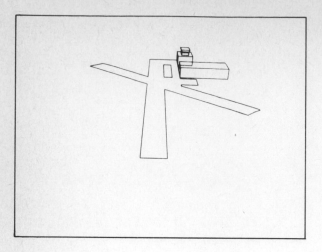

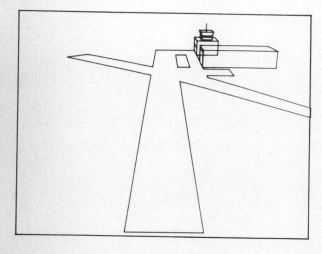

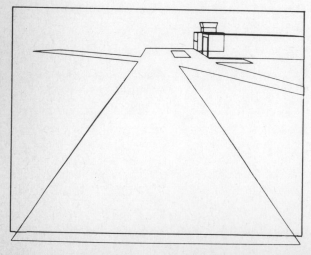

Pictures generated with the "Hi-camper"-programme devised by Sherwood A. Anderson on an IBM 1130/2250 stand-alone system.

Sherwood A. Anderson, 1974/USA.

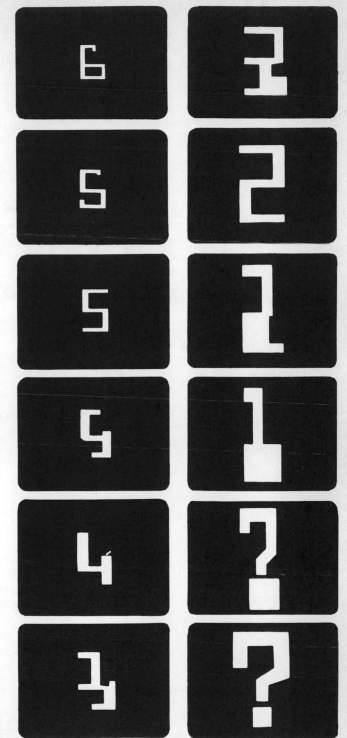

Countdown title sequence for the Halas & Batchelor production "What Is A Computer?".

Computer-Graphics: Tony Pritchett, Direction: Stan Hayward, 1970/GB.

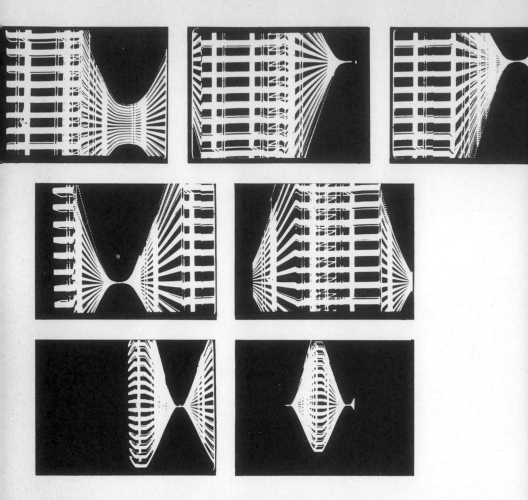

"Scanimate" is a system evolved by Computer Image Corporation in Denver, USA, followed by *"System IV"*, an even faster and more adaptable system for graphic designers.

A promotional production for steel construction by Computer Image Corporation, 1970/USA.

Station logo for ABC-TV, New York, produced with the "Luminetics" System.

Art Direction: Harry Marks, Robert Abel, Design: Wayne Kimbell, 1976/USA.

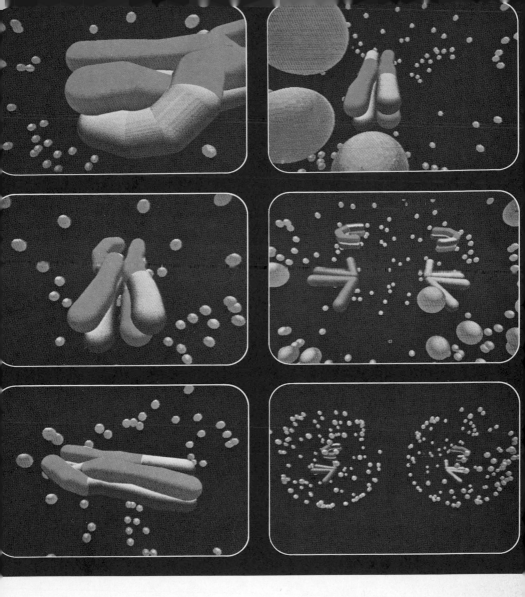

"Synthavision" System by Mathematical Application Graphics (USA, 1976).

Professor Guenther Tetz (University of Illinois, Chicago) is a pioneer in graphical manipulation on screens in real time. 1–3 Modifications with the image processor, 1978. 4–6 Three-dimensional representations, 1978.

Guenther Tetz, Chicago/USA.

Station logo.

Art Direction: Harry Marks, Robert Abel, Design: Wayne Kimbell, 1976/USA.

The production required the creation of only 160 key drawings which, when processed through the system, became 18,000 individual digitized computer images. The specially developed computer animation system is economically rewarding, as well as opening up new potential for artistic expression. "Dilemma", 1981.

*New horizons have been opened up by the fully animated computer graphics film "Dilemma",
a film about the development of civilization and its consequences. "Dilemma", 1981.*

Sequences evolve from close-ups of heads to situations of hostile confrontation. Each metamorphic episode consists of 48 individual phases which were programmed direct onto a digitized pad. "Dilemma", 1981.

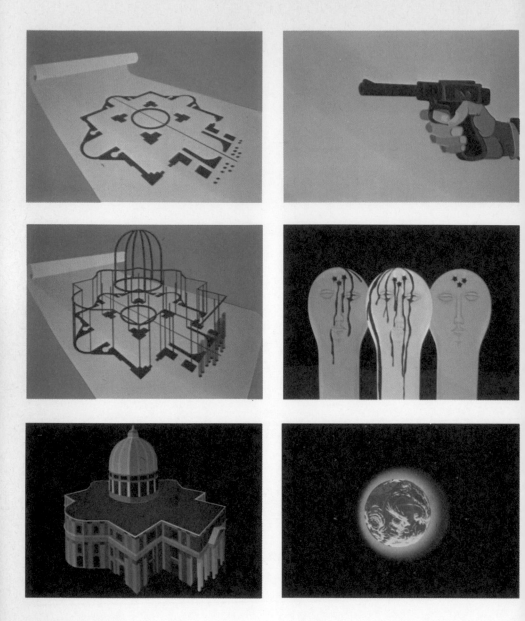

"Dilemma", 1981.

Design: Janos Kass, Computer Direction: Eric Brown, Production: Halas & Batchelor, Educational Film Centre/GB and Computer Creations/USA. Direction/Production: John Halas/GB.

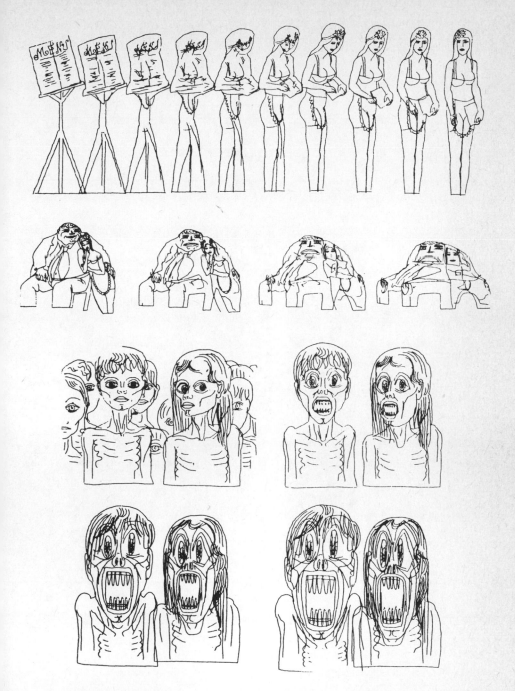

"Hunger" by Peter Földes. The NRC System allows rapid assessment of motion and timing for sequences on the cathode ray tube display.

Computer: N. Bortnyk/M. Wein f. National Film Board of Canada, 1976.

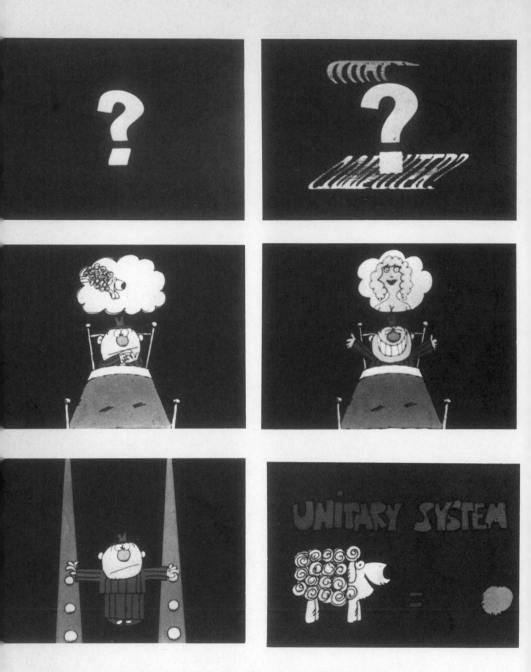

A sequence from Halas & Batchelor's film "What Is A Computer?" (1970) with the opening appropriately processed by a digital computer.

Direction: Stan Hayward, Production: John Halas, 1970/GB.

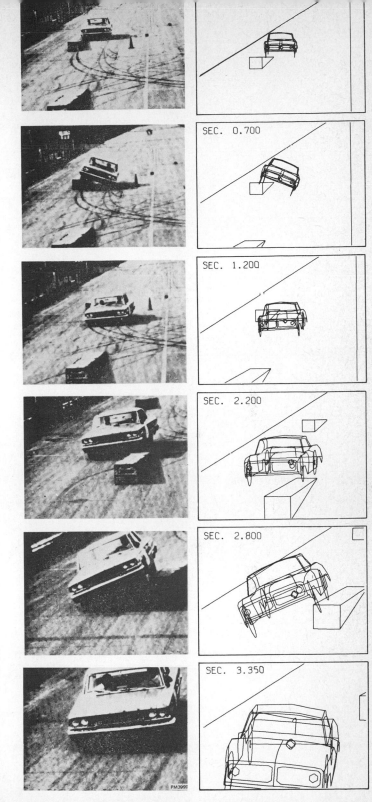

SEC. 0.700

SEC. 1.200

SEC. 2.200

SEC. 2.800

SEC. 3.350

PM3999

"Astro Spiral Jump". A series of computer generated experiments of car responses in dangerous situations.
1 Experiment
2 Computer prediction.

R. R. McHenry, Calspan Corporation, 1974/USA.

Holography
and Laser Graphics

Lasers (Light Amplification by Stimulated Emission of Radiation) have been known for some time now and have become a well-developed and understood technology. The idea was initiated by the Hungarian scientist Denis Gabor in 1949 when he worked in the physics department of British Thomson-Houston Research-Laboratories in Rugby where scientists were encouraged to create three-dimensional movies. As it happened, instead of movies the system became three-dimensional static photography. Denis Gabor perfected his invention at the Imperial College in London in 1966 and by that time Holoco, which started as a special effects process, evolved into a complex three-dimensional image forming system acquiring the name of Holography.

From a modest beginning the exposure and utilisation of laser graphics has become spectacular. The Munich opera festival was an excellent location to present this novel idea of manipulation with special light effects. Quick to apply it on stage, Josef Swoboda incorporated it in his set designs as an experiment for the production of Mozart's "Magic Flute". The floating graphic laser light effects were impressive and since then the system has become a standard tool in stagecraft and choreography for ballets whenever a dramatic impression has to be created.

Both in the USA and in Great Britain special shows have been designed with animated laser lights and presented to large audiences. But the most daring presentation took place at a special exhibition at the Royal Academy of Art in London under the overall title of "Light Fantastic" attracting the attention of all age groups.

Basically, a laser is a device for producing a very pure, coherent, easily controllable, narrow beam of light. The light is emitted by excited electrons bound to the atoms of a solid or gas. These electrons need some initial stimulus to make them emit light,

hence "stimulated emission". Commercial lasers are obtainable which can give light of any colour at will. It is also possible to control and manipulate the intensity and direction of the light beam to a high degree of accuracy. The deflection of a laser beam is accomplished either by mirrors or piezo-electric crystals. Such lasers are known as modulated deflected lasers.

During its short period of existence the laser has been used successfully to create visual effects not only in show places but in architecture, medicine and scientific research. With its tonal shades, laser light has been applied to highlight certain dramatic effects and has assisted in achieving a mood of lyricism and poetry. The light is of extreme colour purity confined to a sharp colour beam. This purity cannot be achieved at such an intensity by any other light source. Incidental animation which appears in three-dimensional space in the theatre can produce interference of great visual beauty. An endless variety of light configurations may be introduced in order to stimulate a sense of participation in the audience.

The graphic designer, in this context the designer of light effects, can repeat his light figures at any time. The laser equipment can be manipulated, once the solution has been found by trial and error with the director of a play. No hard rules should be laid down, only the basic characteristics of the actual light effects; the final happening could be left to the incidental and spontaneous performance of the laser equipment itself. Such light performances, with their rhythms and utilisations of time and space, are expanded to audio-visual presentations and experimental shows to create moving abstract patterns.

Another use of lasers is to draw directly onto film, similar to Norman McLaren's hand-painted film technique. The colour and intensity of the beam is easily changed and optical sound tracks can be recorded directly onto film. Laser cutting tools are utilized to produce animation cut-outs or mattes to a very high degree of accuracy. Futuristic applications might include storing images in the lattice planes of a crystal stimulated by a laser beam; the picture can in turn be projected back by the same laser. By continually rotating the crystal, a sequence of pictures is stored to give the illusion of movement. This arrangement is in effect a shutterless projection machine, since each picture does not appear until the crystal is in the exact orientation. In this way, a single crystal could store say, a thirty-second film for about 50,000 years.

So far, holography has been restricted to still pictures but during the last few years it was also put to use for the production of motion pictures. It is still restricted to only less than one minute of running time, but no doubt with larger models than those in use now, the duration will be extended.

At present, the system requires the light beam generated by the laser and its ability to split it into a reference and object beam. The laser beam illuminates the subject which can be a graphic object or a live person in motion, reflecting the beam onto a photographic film. The same piece of film also collects the reference beam. When the two beams merge an interference pattern bends the light and a three-dimensional reconstruction of the subject appears. Since the light must be coherent, and the light waves must be the same length travelling at the same speed in a parallel direction, only the laser equipment has so far been able to provide the necessary technology for this system.

When developed on a small translucent film, the holographic film looks entirely inconspicuous. It only comes to life when placed in a cylinder (approximately 25×42 mm in diameter) and illuminated from within and below and rotated by means of a motor. By that motion the stereoscopic effect can be observed. The impression of three-dimensionality is due to the fact that the two consecutive frames from the stereo pair can be observed simultaneously with a third of a degree between them as they rotate in the cylinder.

The effects of holograms and laser generated images are dazzling. One is able to walk around a holographic set-up and view it to the extent of 360°. When the viewer moves, the image appears to move as he walks around the image. It floats in space and yet you can put your hand right through it. When the viewer stops, the image stops.

The artists Anait (Los Angeles) and David Ehrlich (New York) have done interesting holographic films and so has Salvador Dali who experimented with lights and motion when he photographed the rock singer Alice Cooper. Since it is now possible to view holographic pictures by using ordinary incandescent light bulbs, one can expect a rapid expansion of the technique both in the direction of moving graphic experiments as well as in new forms of entertainment films.

The area where the laser offers greatest potential is in computer animation. First of all, one must direct the laser at the particular picture or image of interest. This can be done either by way of a suitable scanning technique, whereby the narrow beam of the laser looks at each tiny segment of the image in turn, or by expanding the laser beam into a cone shape which illuminates all of the image simultaneously. A standard television camera picks up the image illuminated by the laser and so gives a picture on a television monitor.

Until recently, the next step has run into several problems, notably a lack of economic storage space inside the computer and a difficulty in "wiring up" or interfacing a laser or a television camera to a computer. However, research over the last few years in the field of charge coupled devices (CCD) promises to eliminate these difficulties. Newer technology provides a method of making memory elements on a very small silicon crystal which, highly magnified, has an actual size of about 0.115" × 0.066". These memory elements can be charged either electrically via a computer or by light falling on them. In essence they form a light-sensitive device easily interfaced to a computer and used as a direct replacement for a normal television camera. Owing to CCD technology, it would be possible to build interfaces which will enable a computer to interact with a laser or television camera and store a high definition picture easily and cheaply. CCD devices are very new and as yet unproved. It remains to be seen whether they will fulfil their promise.

Once the image is stored in a computer it can be processed by available techniques. Programmes already exist to move, rotate, scale, in-between and perform some special effects on pictures stored in a computer. Not only can the laser simplify the task of inputting images into a computer, but it can also help to output them after they have been processed by enclosing a modulating laser in a light-proof box and controlling it from a computer. It is possible to draw a picture directly onto 16 or 35 mm film. The computer tells the laser which part of the film to scan, and what colour and intensity to use. The laser then exposes the film which can be developed in the normal way. The laser here replaces the cathode ray tube in conventional microfilm plotters, and the result is of much higher resolution with colour and gray scale achieved instantaneously.

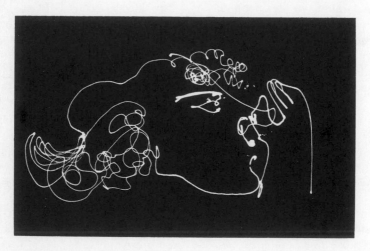

Light Drawings in Space, 1981.

Design: Kaj Franck/SF.

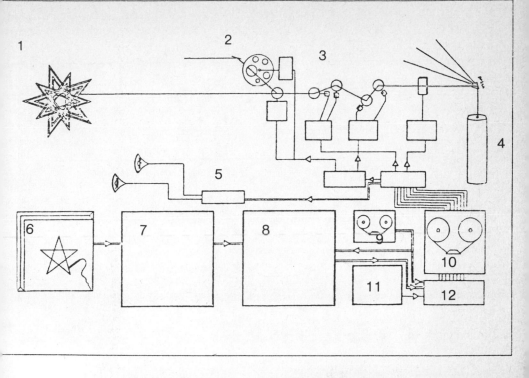

The basic processes of laser graphics. 1 Laser
Art, 2 Deflector, 3 Connectors, 4 Laser,
5 Audio, 6 Electronic Sketch Pad, 7 Digital
Signal Processing, 8 Analog Signal Processing, 9 Sound track, 10 Master Tape Recorder,
11 Logic, 12 Encoding.

Design: John Wolff/GB.

The image formig techniques of laser graphics were made possible by the development of Holography by Professor Dennis Gabor in 1947. Since then, John Wolff has advanced the method into a considerable and exciting aesthetic experience.

Laser sign writing: John Wolff, Nick Phillips, Anton Furst, HOLOCO, Shepperton Studio Centre/GB.

1 Laser generated images for the
presentation of "Love Light"
by John ›Coco‹ Montague
of General Scanning Inc./USA,
2 "The Brain Behind the Laser Light
Show".

1 Design: Gred Stern, Production:
Metropole Laser Theatre, London/GB,
2 Design: John Wolff, Production:
HOLOCO, Shepperton Studio Centre/GB.

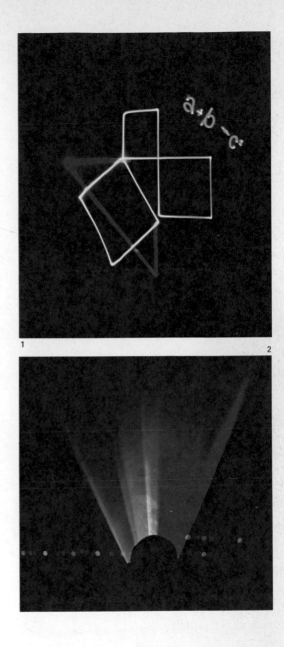

1

2

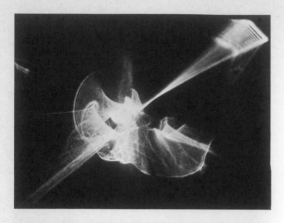

Laser graphics for the Cosmic Laser Concert "Laserium", presented at the London Planetarium.

Design: Ivan Dryer, Production: Laser Images Inc., Van Nuys, Calif./USA.

"Laserium", a Cosmic Laser Concert. The use of laser technology expanded into a theatrical and special visual concert, both in Los Angeles and in London. The floating, three-dimensional, visual effects of dazzling coloured lights and forms rising freely in space, no longer need the confined silver screen or TV cathode ray tube. A new age may have dawned for graphic conceptions.

Design: Ivan Dreyer/GB.

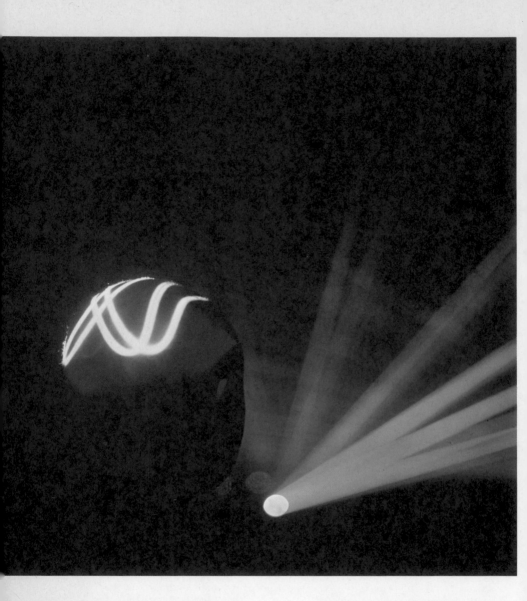

"The Brain Behind the Laser Light Show".

Design: John Wolff, Production:
HOLOCO, Shepperton Studio Centre/GB.

The "Love Light" laser light concert ▷
which has been presented in USA, Great
Britain, France and Germany in the last
few years.

John ›Coco‹ Montague, General Scanning Incorporated/USA, Design: Gred
Stern.

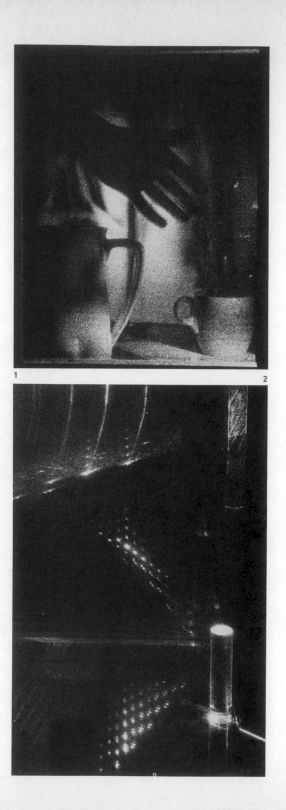

1

2

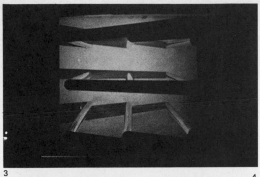

1 This hologram shows currents of hot air invisible to the naked eye and a non-hologram of a hand. Anything that moves more than a fraction of a wave length will not record. The hand in the hologram has not recorded and appears paradoxically as a solid "hole" or three-dimensional silhouette.

2 A direct laser beam reflected by a set of parallel glass plates is multiplied into many points of light. A normal source would only reflect once.

3 The image of metal rods comes right up against the holographic plate casting shadows on its surface. Parallax motion is emphasized in viewing the plate.

4 An attempt has been made to widen the angle by spreading the beam over two holographic plates. By using holographic film made into a cylinder it is possible to achieve an "all-round" view of an object.

Margaret Benyon/GB.

3

4

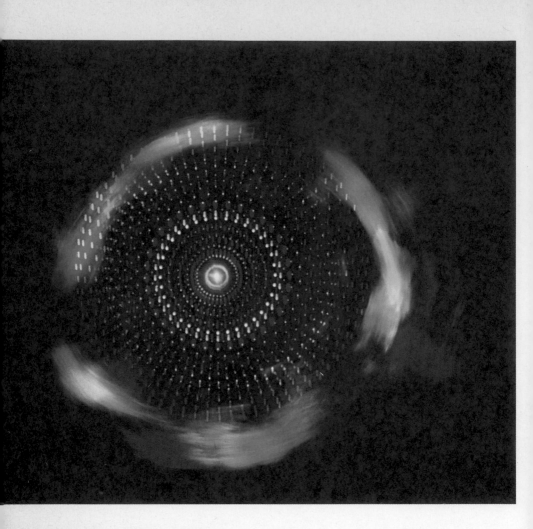

The Cosmic Laser Concert "Laserium".

Design: Ivan Dryer, Production: Laser Images
Inc./USA.

M. Benyon has made a unique contribution with holographic and stereoscopic graphic experiments, and is one of the pioneers, being able to combine creative expression with engineering technology.

1 A double-exposure hologram. By exposing the plate to two different set-ups, it is possible to achieve the appearance of "weightlessness".
2 Holographic picture.
3 A triple-exposure hologram. Three separate images can be seen as the plate is turned through 60°. The hologram gives more information than is possible with a two-dimensional photograph, as one is able to look round the sides of the object. "Holographic Graphics".

Margaret Benyon/GB.

1

2

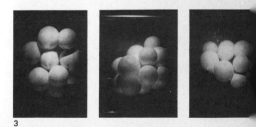

3

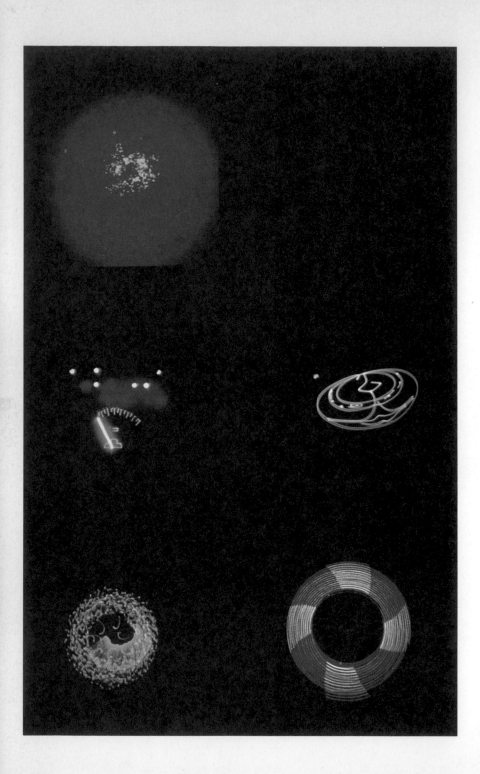

172

Further examples of laser light used to achieve figure and colour pattern designs.

John ›Coco‹ Montague, General Scanning Inc./USA, Design: Gred Stern.

The "Love Light" laser light concert which has been presented in USA, Great Britain, France and Germany in the last few years.

John ›Coco‹ Montague, General Scanning Incorporated/USA, Design: Gred Stern.

Interplay of Image, Sound and Lettering in Films

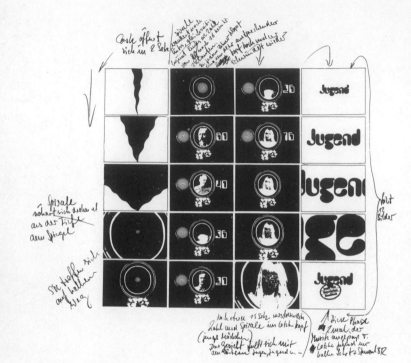

In the previous chapters, I have tried to provide an insight into the range of activities in motion graphics up to the present stage of development they have reached. In the following, I would like to deal with certain limitations of this medium and some rules which should be observed if a production is to succeed.

A unity must be established between the moving picture and the sound if the film is to create a total impression backed by an aural experience. The sound track may consist of dialogue or commentary, music or sound effects, or a combination of all these elements. If image and sound are adequately co-ordinated effects will be achieved that emphasize the points to be made or help establish any mood required.

Under no circumstances should a film production be started without a storyboard. Planned to the last detail it shows the essential flow of continuity. It points out the visual development of each individual shot as well as the scene changes while indicating the angles of each character, their shapes and the relationship between the pictorial content and the sound track. Technical instructions are also helpful. Not only are all aspects of the problems to be solved during the production revealed from the very beginning — the entire scope of a project can be planned ahead safely.

One of the factors to bear in mind which distinguishes a film from other media is that a moving picture must be kept moving. Unlike static graphics, it is subjected to a time schedule and assumes a spacial dimension. As may have been gathered, even making comic strip cartoons, which might also contain a number of drawings arranged in continuity, proves to be far less complicated than creating a film. Movement imposes its demands because it has a beginning and an end as well as the time units in between these extreme points. Depending on the effects to be achieved, impressions can be imparted that range from soft lyricism to forceful dynamism. What is inconceivable in other forms of design activity, e. g. a single picture, becomes possible: time continuity can be treated as an additional creative element.

With the exception of abstract and special visual effects, when designing a character for a moving picture, an animated figure is used. The latter must be clearly defined, leaving no doubt as to what type is to be represented. Besides, it should be extremely simply drawn and easily reproducible for the repetitious hand animation or when processed in one of the recent electronic systems. A characteristic voice helps to vivify the drawn model even more. In contrast to a live actor, such an animated figure will give immediate clues as to its nature by exaggerated features, such as eyes, nose, and body proportions. In other words, it becomes totally functional in the medium for which it is created.

The same sense of exaggeration and emphasis can be applied to an object or to a static shape since, thanks to various devices, it is possible to distort, squeeze, elongate and squash a form no matter what its original shape is. This capacity of motion graphics is especially rewarding when it comes to the presentation of moving lettering, trade marks, and the introduction of products in a promotional film for television. The choreography of moving lettering integrated with the close-up of a pack design could emphasize a well-known trade mark. With the backing of an imaginative sound track this could become a very powerful visual tool to be impressed on the minds of an audience for a very long time. Here is the basic value of combining as many elements of the existing tricks at the disposal of the graphic designer.

As we have seen, the creation of a motion picture, whether it is hand- or machinemade, is very expensive and extremely complex, especially in view of the latest technologies available. It is essential to integrate the various elements, such as design and production methods, into the overall presentation of the product which will govern the successful execution of a programme. Here is a summary for consideration:

1. Good, clear, creative design as the basis of a project.

2. The sequential and logical development of a complete story or a happening in an acceptable visual continuity.

3. The creation of a storyboard in which any alterations could be made before starting a production.

4. A script with meaningful text, establishing a relationship between dialogue, commentary and moving picture. Words should not be duplicated with pictures, for they cancel each other out.

5. The creation of music and sound effects as an integral part of the motion continuity, helping to emphasize a point or counter point, and to accentuate mood.

6. The all encompassing knowledge of methods and techniques in order to choose which one to use for a specific assignment.

The integration of movement into close-up with the design of trade mark lettering and live action could have a powerful impression.
1 Moving text "Zwiesel" from a TV commercial/D.
2 From a TV commercial for "Rowi" advertising a wrist watch.

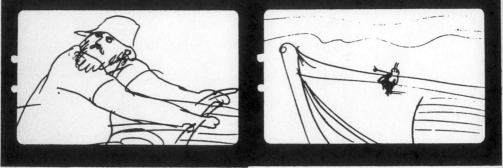

A storyboard is essential to establish a clear flowing continuity and the relationship between visuals and words. It is also for making corrections as one develops the story. "Gunnar Karlson's 'Dunderklumpen'", 1972.

Design: Per Ahlin, Production: GK-Film Studio/S.

Part of a storyboard from "1001 Arabian Nights" by the successful producer/director Osamu ▷ Tezuka, 1973/J.

An integrated campaign between televison advertising and newspaper advertisements. Using the same logotypes and lettering with related layouts could be highly valuable.
From a TV programme "Bravo", a tele-novel about a conductor and a pianist by Globo TV/BR.

Design: Hans-Jürgen Donner/Via Trenker, 1969.

Conclusion

Few professions have been confronted with such dramatic changes as that of graphic design in this century. Its scope has been enlarged from the printed to many other media, most of them entirely new industries. Apart from advertising, publishing, and typography it can be closely involved with scientific information and research, sign languages, international symbols, mathematics, physics, chemistry, biology, electronics, cybernetics and communications systems just to list some of the new areas of graphic design activity. The invention of audio-visual, TV, video and other electronic equipment also requires an understanding of complex problems.

As a consequence of this technical advance graphic designers can acquire a view of a far wider dimension than in the past. Communication design, which is a practice most of them are involved with today, need no longer be the frontier of their creative work. On the contrary, in our visually orientated society the graphic designer may become an essential contributor in the building of our future world and an interpreter of our complex technology, while presenting a new international language he himself has developed.

There are certain ethical obligations for this profession that should not be disregarded. One is to demolish the more or less hard border lines still existing between science and professional training as well as between fine arts and graphic arts. For in a society, where the creative human mind and "machine intelligence" are of the same world the cardinal rule should be mutual respect and joint action.

HEAD IS
2/3. OF HEIGHT

Functionally designed figures with exaggerated features have an instand impact on audiences. Final artwork and character design for "Marathon".

Design: Johnny Hart, Production: Samuel Magdoff, 1971/USA.

Appendix

Key to abbreviations

AUS	Australia	D	Germany	NL	Netherlands
B	Belgium	F	France	PL	Poland
BG	Bulgaria	GB	Great Britain	SF	Finland
CDN	Canada	H	Hungary	SU	Soviet Union
CH	Switzerland	I	Italy	USA	United States of America
CS	Czechoslovakia	J	Japan	YU	Yugoslavia

Bibliography

Anderson, Yvonne Make Your Own Animated Movies: Yellow Ball Workshop Film Techniques. Boston, Little Brown, 1970.

Arnheim, Rudolf Art and Visual Perception. Berkeley, University of California Press, 1965.

Arnheim, Rudolf Visual Thinking. Berkeley, University of California Press, 1974.

Asenin, Serge The Animated Picture. Moscow Publishing, 1974.

Bendazzi, Gianalberto Topolino e Poi. Mailand, Edizioni Il Formichiere, 1979.

Bocek, Jaroslav Jiri Trnka: Artist and Puppet Master. Prag, Artia, 1965.

Cabarga, Leslie The Fleischer Story. New York, Crown, 1976.

Collins, Maynard Norman McLaren. Canadian Film Institute, 1976.

Field, Robert The Art of Walt Disney. New York, McMillan, 1942.

Halas, John Visual Scripting. London, Focal Press, 1973.

Halas, John Computer Animation. London, Focal Press, 1974.

Halas, John Film Animation: A Simplified Approach. Paris, UNESCO, 1977.

Halas, John/Edera, Bruno Full Length Animated Feature Films. New York, Hastings House; Focal Press, London, 1977.

Halas, John/Herdeg, Walter Film and TV Graphics 1. Zürich: Graphis Press, 1967.

Halas, John/Herdeg, Walter Film and TV Graphics 2. Zürich, Graphis Press, 1976.

Halas, John/Manvell, Roger The Technique of Film Animation. London, Focal Press, 1968.

Halas, John/Manvell, Roger Art in Movement: New Directions in Animation. London, Studio Vista, 1970.

Halas, John/Privett, Bob How To Cartoon. London, Focal Press, 1955.

Halas, John/Rider, David The Great Movie Cartoon Parade. New York, Bounty Books, 1976.

Hausen, Ray Harry Film Fantasy Scrapbook. New York, Barnes, 1972.

Hayward, Stan Scriptwriting for Animation. New York, Hastings House; London. Focal Press, 1978.

Heraldson, Donald Creators of Life: A History of Animation. New York, Drake, 1975.

Holloway, Ronald Z is for Zagreb. New York, Barnes, 1972.

Jungstedt, Torsten Kapten Grogg och Hans Vanner. Stockholm, Sveriges Radios Forlag, 1973.

Kinoshita, Renzo Japanese Animation Directors. Kinoshita, Tokio, 1979.

Levitan, Eli Animation Art in the Commercial Film. New York, Reinhold, 1960.

Lutz, Edwin George Animated Cartoons: How they are made: Their Origin and Development. New York, Gordon Press, 1976.

Madsen, Roy P. Animated Films: Concepts, Methods, Uses. New York, Interland, 1969.

Maelstaf, R. The Animated Cartoon Film in Belgium, Brussels, Ministry of Foreign Affairs, 1970.

Manvell, Roger The Animated Film. New York, Hastings House, 1954.

Manvell, Roger Animation. 15th edition, 1974.

Manvell, Roger Art and Animation. London, Tantivy Press, 1980.

McLaren, Norman Cameraless Animation. National Film Board of Canada, 1958.

McLaren, Norman The Drawings of Norman McLaren. Montreal, Tundra Books, 1975.

Muybridge, Eadweard Animals in Motion und The Human Figure in Motion. New York, Dover, 1955/56.

Perisic, Zoran The Animation Stand. New York, Hastings House, London, Focal Press, 1976.

Reiniger, Lotte Shadow Theatres and Shadow Films. New York, Watson Guptill, 1970.

Rondolio, Gianni Storia del Cinema d'Animazione. Turin, Giulio Einaudi Editore, 1974.

Salt, Brian G. D. Movements in Animation. Oxford, Pergammon Press, 1976.

Salt, Brian G. D. Basic Animation Stand Techniques. Oxford, Pergammon Press, 1977.

Schickel, Richard The Disney Version. New York, Avon, 1968. London, Weidenfeld & Nicholson, 1968.

Whitaker, Harold/Halas, John Timing for Animation. London, Focal Press, 1981.

Whitney, John Digital Harmony. Peterborough, New Hampshire, Byte Books/McGraw-Hill Publications, 1980.

Willener, Alfred Guy Milliard and Alex Ganty; translated and revised by Diana Burfield, Videology and Utopia. London, Routledge and Kegan Paul, 1976.

List of Names

All figures are page numbers
Page references in upright type
Illustration references in italics

Index

All figures are page numbers
Page references in upright type
Illustration references in italics

Illustration credits

Reference to inserted title vignettes:
7 "Birds Bees and Storks", John Halas/Gerard Hoffnung, 1964/GB – 15 "Learning to Walk", Borivoj Dovniković, 1976/YU – 105 „Per Aspera ad Astra", Nedeljko Dragić, 1971/YU – 129 "Opens Wednesday", Barrie Nelson, 1980/USA – 157 "Tales of Hoffnung", John Halas/Gerard Hoffnung, 1965/GB – 175 "Linear Programming", John Halas/Harold Whitaker, 1971/GB – 178 "Skyrider", John Halas, 1971/GB.

The data given below refer to the number, year and page of the novum issue from which the illustration is taken.

16 Direction: John Canemaker, Phoenix Film – 19 Dirk Deparfe – 20 From: John Halas/Roger Manvell "Art and Movement", Studio Vistra, London 1970 – 21 Design: Roger Mainwood, Production: Halas & Batchelor – 22 From: John Halas "Film Animation: A Simplified Approach", UNESCO 1976 – 23 Fig. 1, 2: No. 11, 1977, p. 23; Fig. 3: No. 11, 1978, p. 36 – 24 No. 1, 1977, p. 46 – 25 No. 1, 1977, p. 47 – 26 Design: Frank Mouris, Frank Film, 1975 – 27 No. 11, 1978, p. 32 – 28 Fig. 1–3: p. 7, 1977, p. 45; Fig. 4: p. 7, 1979, 20 – 29 p. 11, 1978, p. 35 – 30 p. 7, 1977, p. 40 – 31 No. 11, 1978, p. 36 – 32 Fig. 1: Bob Godfrey Films, Fig. 2: Gerrit van Dijk – 33 No. 5, 1975, p. 14 – 34 No. 7, 1979, p. 24 – 35 Design: Pavao Stalter – 36 Design: Peter Sis, Production/Direction: John Halas – 37 Design: Peter Sis, Production/Direction: John Halas – 38 Sandor Reisenbuckler, Pannonia Film – 39 No. 3, 1977, p. 47 – 40 No. 11, 1978, p. 37 – 41 No. 11, 1978, p. 34 – 42 No. 2, 1975, p. 22 – 43: Fig. 1–4: No. 12, 1980, p. 25; Fig. 5–7: No. 9, 1977, p. 53 – 44 Nedeljko Dragić, Zagreb Film – 45 No. 11, 1978, p. 31 – 46 Fig. 1, 2 Design: Alan Aldridge, Fig. 3 Design: Tom Bailley, Production: Halas & Batchelor – 47 Fig. 1: Giselle Ansorge, Fig. 2: Ferenc Rofusz – 48 Fig. 1: Borge Ring, Fig. 2: Bretislav Pojar – 49 Direction: John Halas, Halas & Batchelor – 50 Fig. 1: No. 11, 1978, p. 34; Fig. 2: No. 11, 1978, p. 30 – 51 No. 11, 1977, p. 28 – 52 No. 5, 1975, p. 16 – 53 Fig. 1 Direction: John Hubley, Fig. 2 Direction: Tony White – 54 No. 12, 1980, p. 26 – 55 Fig. 1–3: No. 11, 1977, p. 27; Fig. 4–6: No. 11, 1977, p. 22 – 56 Design: Ronald Searle, Production: Halas & Batchelor – 57 Fig. 1 Design: Ginger Gibbons, Gillian Lacey; Fig. 2 Design: Geoff Dunbar, Production: Halas & Batchelor – 58 No. 9, 1977, p. 55 – 59 No. 3, 1977, p. 41 – 60 Design: Alan Aldridge, Halas & Batchelor – 61 No. 3, 1977, p. 3 – 62 Fig. 1–3, 5: No. 9, 1977, p. 52; Fig. 4: No. 9, 1974, p. 36 – 63 Fig. 1–5: No. 2, 1981, p. 31; Fig. 6, 7: No. 11, 1977, p. 28 – 64 No. 3, 1977, 38 – 65 No. 3, 1977, p. 42 – 66 No. 7, 1979, p. 23 – 67 No. 9, 1974, p. 45 – 68 Fig. 1: No. 9, 1977, p. 51; Fig. 2, 3: No. 9, 1977, p. 56; Fig. 4, 5: No. 9, 1977, p. 52 – 69 No. 2, 1981, p. 33 – 70 No. 9, 1974, p. 37 – 71 Design: Jean Pierre Jacquet – 72/73 No. 2, 1975, p. 20 – 74 Fig. 1: José Xavier, Fig. 2: Joško Marušić, Fig. 3: Chris James – 75 No. 11, 1978, p. 33 – 76 No. 9, 1974, p. 40 – 77 Fig. 1: No. 9, 1974, p. 37; Fig. 2, 3: No. 9, 1974, p. 36 – 78 No. 12, 1980, p. 27 – 80 No. 10, 1979, p. 10 – 83 Süddeutscher Rundfunk, 1974 – 84 No. 5, 1977, p. 38 – 85 No. 11, 1975, p. 12 – 86 No. 10, 1979, p. 10 – 87 No. 10, 1979, p. 3 – 88 No. 5, 1975, p. 17 – 89 No. 8, 1975, p. 6 – 90 No. 11, 1978, p. 42 – 91 No. 11, 1978, p. 42 – 92 No. 5, 1975, p. 2 – 93 No. 5, 1975, p. 5 – 94 Fig. 1: No. 5, 1975, p. 15; Fig. 2: No. 5, 1975, p. 14; Fig. 3: No. 5, 1975, p. 16 – 95 No. 5, 1978, p. 5 – 96 No. 5. 1975, p. 8 – 97 Liz Friedmann, BBC TV – 98/99 Stewart Austin, BBC TV – 100 No. 1, 1978, p. 32 – 101 No. 1, 1978, p. 29, 31 – 102 No. 1, 1978, p. 29 – 103 Production: Halas & Batchelor, 1978 – 104 Production: Halas & Batchelor, 1973 – 108 No. 10, 1976, p. 37 – 109 Design: Richard Monkhouse, William Kentish – 110 No. 5, 1977, p. 39 – 111 No. 10, 1976, p. 38 – 112 No. 8, 1975, p. 4 – 113 No. 8, 1975, p. 4 – 114 No. 10, 1976, p. 38 – 115 No. 11, 1975, p. 8 – 116 No. 9, 1974, p. 44 – 117 No. No., 1975, p. 4 – 118 No. 11, 1975, p. 8 – 119 No. 10, 1976, p. 39 – 120 No. 3, 1980, p. 14 – 121 No. 3, 1980, p. 14 – 122 No. 2, 1981, p. 30 – 123 No. 8, 1976, p. 20 – 124 No. 2, 1980, p. 42 – 125 No. 10, 1979, p. 7 – 126 No. 10, 1979, p. 11 – 127 No. 10, 1979, p. 6 – 133 No. 8, 1976, p. 17 – 135 Fig. 1 Simulation: Robert Abel, Fig. 2 Design: Eric Brown – 136 No. 8, 1976, p. 17 – 137 Lillian F. Schwartz, Charles B. Rubinstein – 138 Lillian F. Schwartz, Charles B. Rubinstein – 139 Fig. 1 Direction: John Halas, Joy Batchelor; Fig. 2 Computer graphics: Brian Borthwick, John Halas – 140 Lillian F. Schwartz – 141 Courtesy of IBM-INFORMATIQUE – 142 Sherwood A. Anderson – 143 Computer graphics Tony Pritchett, Direction: Stan Hayward – 144 Computer Image Corporation, USA – 145 No. 8, 1976, p. 21 – 146 No. 7, 1976, p. 39 – 147 No. 7, 1976, p. 42 – 148 No. 8, 1976, p. 21 – 149 No. 6, 1981, p. 14 – 150 No. 6, 1981, p. 16, 17 – 151 No. 6, 1981, p. 16 – 152 No. 6, 1981, p. 14, 15 – 153 Computer: N. Bortnyk, M. Wein – 154 Direction: Stan Hayward, Production: John Halas – 155 No. 11, 1975, p. 7 – 160 Kaj Franck – 161 Design: John Wolff – 162 No. 6, 1978, p. 10 – 163 No. 6, 1978, p. 12 – 164 No. 6, 1978, p. 11 – 165 Design: Ivan Dreyer – 166 No. 6, 1978, p. 12 – 167 No. 6, 1978, p. 13 – 168/169 No. 11, 1975, p. 15 – 170 No. 6, 1978, p. 12 – 171 No. 11, 1975, p. 15 – 172 No. 6, 1978, p. 13 – 173 No. 6, 1978, p. 13 – 176 From "Gebrauchswörterbuch Fernsehen", published by Bayerischer Rundfunk 1972; Design/Graphics: Günter Griebl – 179 From: Erhardt D. Stiebner/Walter Leonhard "Bruckmann's Handbuch der Schrift", 2nd Edition, München 1980, p. 192/193 – 180 Design: Per Ahlin, Production: GK-Film Studio – 181 Direction/Production: Osamu Tezuka – 182 Design: Hans-Jürgen Donner, Via Trenker – 184 Design: Johnny Hart, Production: Samuel Magdoff